An Elite Journey

A Young Man's Leadership Story

Written By
Michael Massucci

Attitude · Excellence · Others
AEO Leadership LLC

An Elite Journey: A Young Man's Leadership Story
November 2014

Copyright©2014 by Michael L. Massucci
Published by
    AEO Leadership, LLC
    Royal Oak, Michigan 48073
    coachmassucci@gmail.com

Summary: *An Elite Journey: A Young Man's Leadership Story* is a coming of age story of a young athlete and the lessons he learns playing the game he loves. The story embraced in this book is intended to be a work of fiction. Any reference to any historical events or real people is used fictitiously and is entirely coincidental.

ISBN 978-0-692-30188-3
Edited by Chris Lewis and Jan Wetzel
Printed by Clark Graphics, Inc., Troy, Michigan

Price: In US $13.95

Acknowledgements

First and foremost I would like to thank my wife Karen and my three sons AJ, Anthony, and Jake for all of their help in writing this book. Karen is an inspiring woman who has helped me become a better person, coach, and teacher. What a gift it is to have a family that believes in you and supports you. You four mean the world to me, and I could not have completed this story without you.

I would also like to thank my parents Art and Mimi, for their guidance and help. It is a true blessing to have parents that support you unconditionally. I would like to thank my brother Marty, my sister Amy, and their spouses for all their help through this process. Marty, has been a great assistant coach for me for many years, and my sister Amy, is the best teacher I know. Their children, my nieces and nephews, especially Brennan, all contributed in the editing and revising of this book. This was a true team effort.

I would like to give a special thank you to Tim McCormick and Mike Dietz, the cofounders of the Michigan Elite 25 Program. Simply put, the E25

Brotherhood has changed the lives of hundreds, soon to be thousands of young basketball players in Michigan. Many of the quotes, anecdotes, and stories come directly from my experiences working with Tim. He is a valued friend and one of the best leaders and motivational speakers I know.

Also, a special thanks to Dan Wetzel for writing the foreword. He is one of the most recognizable and important names in sports today, and his support and friendship are much appreciated.

Though this story is fictional, the storyline and many of the characters are based on over 20 years of coaching varsity basketball. This book is dedicated to all of my players and students, past and present. I have been blessed to coach and teach such outstanding young people. Promise to always "choose the hard right over the easy wrong."

Table of Contents

Foreword

At any age we seek a game plan for life, words of wisdom and motivation that can sharpen our focus on what's important. It helps first to define our true goals and then assist in an attempt to accomplish them.

This is particularly important during the formative years of youth, when the frivolity of childhood fades and a confusing present takes over as everyone eyes an uncertain future. It's also known as high school. It's easy to say you seek success, but what does that mean? And how to do make it a reality?

Make the team. Make the shot. Make the grade. Yet even that isn't everything. Even that can leave you empty.

For over two decades now Michael Massucci has been known in Michigan as a great basketball coach. He currently leads Royal Oak High School outside of Detroit and via the Elite 25, works each summer with the very best players from across the state.

He's coached every type of kid, from future college All Americans and NBA champions to the last man on the bench who needed the daily structure of practice to find his footing academically and socially.

He's also, a dedicated teacher and to those of us that know him best, a devoted husband and father of three boys, each a relentless athlete in their own right.

He's one of those glues to a community, always coaching and teaching someone, somewhere, even when they may not realize it. Sometimes, it's just by quietly showing the way through his actions. He is, additionally, a man of deep faith, which unquestionably guides his every move.

There couldn't have been a better marriage of author and topic than Michael and a how-to guide for self-motivation of a young athlete. It's like his entire life has built to this book, a chance to impact more kids and parents than his team or classroom possibly could fit.

An Elite Journey is first about the challenges that Michael has recognized and fought through with his players for years, complete with the effective solution that has proven to work time and time again.

I've spent my career talking to, interviewing and observing successful athletes, coaches and businessmen in the world of sports. From LeBron James to Peyton Manning to Tiger Woods to Bill Belichick to Calvin Johnson to Tom Izzo to Michael Phelps to Phil Knight and so on, there so often common themes of focus, faith and finding the courage to carve one's own path. They are stronger mentally and emotionally than they are physically, suggesting they could've been a success in any walk of life they chose. Yet each, on a daily basis, is always striving for more in the never-ending pursuit of fulfilling potential.

There is a dearth of these kinds of books, focused on high school kids, particularly boys; ones with time honored advice that can refocus even the oldest adult reader. This is what you wish someone told you as your confidence was rocked by the particular challenges of adolescence, from peer pressure, to fearing you aren't good enough to the general wonder at how life can properly be navigated.

There is a depth to the story, from the central characters to the challenges they face, which go beyond just quantitative things like making a free throw and into the intangibles of self worth. It's all there in a fast, page turning read, complete with questions at the end of each chapter to help young minds focus on the message, and the path, presented.

Not everyone is going to be CJ, a gifted athlete with an entire town cheering his every athletic success.

That isn't the point. Everyone can relate to the doubts and hurdles CJ needed to overcome to find a more direct route to the life he wanted to lead and the realization of what is most important in that life. Everyone can follow the plan that helps he or she hit whatever constitutes his or her own personal pressure packed free throw.

This is a user's guide to a young life, brought to you from a coach and teacher and a father who honed his lesson from daily leadership on his court, in his classroom, and throughout his community.

This is a great book. This here is some great stuff.

Dan Wetzel
National Columnist
Yahoo Sports
New York Times best-selling author

Introduction

This is an exciting time in your life, as you are in the middle of an amazing journey. You will learn shortly that success and winning are not random. There is a reason that some players commit to a championship game plan, and they chase incredible goals while others just sit back and hope to reach the next level.

My name is Tim McCormick, and I am excited to write an introduction for *An Elite Journey: A Young Man's Leadership Story.* My background includes McDonald's All-American honors at Clarkston High School, All Big Ten at the University of Michigan, and ten seasons as a player in the NBA.

For the last 20 years, I have served as the camp director of the NBA Players Association's TOP 100 Camp, which has helped develop over 150 current NBA players, including Kobe Bryant, Dwight Howard, Kevin Durant, Rajon Rondo, and Kyrie Irving, to name a few. The same professional model that emphasizes academics, basketball fundamentals, life skills development, and high character expectations is available to you throughout this book.

This book is meant to challenge you to make the commitment to rise above the road blocks and career-killers that destroy so many dreams. It will also encourage you adhere to the highest character and academic standards. After reading this book, we encourage you to go back to your schools and provide much needed leadership to your teammates and classmates. Moreover, we want you to be a leader at home and in your community, as you bring out the best in those around you. This book provides the right game plan and gives you the opportunity to become great.

Sincerely,

Tim McCormick
NBA Players Association Top 100 Director
Michigan Elite 25, Camp Director
ESPN Analyst

Prologue

It was the Michigan high school basketball state championship game, and the Knights were playing the mighty Cavaliers in the packed Breslin Center in East Lansing, Michigan. The Knights were down 1 with just 1.8 seconds to play. The Knights' star player, junior CJ Harding, was at the foul line shooting a pressure-filled one and one. CJ had an iron clad routine. He began with one deep breath, then took three dribbles, added one spin, and always said a positive affirmation. He calmly drained the first one, nothing but net.

CJ had one of the purest shots anyone had ever seen. The crowd watched the 16-year-old phenom with amazement. CJ was "in the zone" ready for his second shot, when the opposing coach called a timeout, trying to freeze the young star.

During the Knights' huddle, their coach, Coach Dailey, knowing the psychology of his super-star, simply said, "Trust your training." He knew full well there was nobody more prepared for this moment than his elite guard, CJ Harding. As one famous sports cable announcer might say, he was a "prime time player."

Coach Dailey was a former player himself and a promising young coach. The development of CJ Harding not only made his program one of the state's elite teams, but also raised his profile as a coach. There was nobody who respected and appreciated CJ Harding quite like Coach Dailey.

As the Knights broke the huddle, CJ was focused on his routine. His distraction control was unlike that of any other athlete. This was the state championship; thousands of fans were on the edge of their seats, and the Cavaliers' student section was going crazy. CJ's mom and little sister were covering their eyes, unable to watch as he prepared to shoot another free throw.

There was something special about CJ; he was different than other kids. He had a certain swagger about him; he was cool without being arrogant. He had a sense of destiny about him.

As CJ approached the foul line, he smiled to himself, knowing full well he was prepared for this moment. This shot was not just for his school, his family, his coach, or his teammates. This shot was also for the person most responsible for helping a young kid with a lot of potential, transform into an elite athlete who was ready to seize the moment.

An Elite Journey

A Young Man's Leadership Story

Trey -

Always remember
that leadership is
a choice. Wishing
you the best.

M Massuco
CEO

Chapter 1

Learning Lessons

Two Years Earlier

CJ was in the backseat of his mom's car listening to music during, what seemed to be, the longest car ride ever. He kept agonizingly asking himself, "How could I have missed that last second shot? I was wide open!" His eyes were moist from tears of frustration, as he kept replaying the last play of the game over and over.

"I was wide open," he kept repeating to himself. CJ's worst fear had actually happened. For as long as he had been playing the game of basketball, he was always afraid of making a mistake that would cost his team the game. CJ played in a constant fear of failure. During his team's last timeout and before the last shot of the game, he said to himself, "I better not miss this." He could not believe he actually missed the last shot and blew his opportunity to win the game. How could he face his teammates in school tomorrow?

Although CJ was only a freshman, he played on his high school's junior varsity basketball team. Young and inexperienced, he was taking the Knights' loss very hard, thinking he disappointed his teammates and his coach. Looking at his phone and gazing through his Twitter feed, CJ could already see the comments from his teammates.

"Should've won," tweeted one friend.

"Great season," replied another.

CJ then tweeted without much thought "My bad tonight boys, I hate basketball!!"

Though he liked his teammates, CJ did not care for Coach Malone, who was always negative and screamed obvious statements without much instruction, such as, "Come on, CJ. You have to make your layups!!" Like CJ didn't know that layups were important.

Coach Malone constantly told CJ that he would never amount to anything, that he was too soft, that he did not work hard enough, and that he did not want it bad enough. The most dreaded statement that Coach Malone would scream at CJ, at least once a week, was, "Come on, CJ. You're nothing like your dad." Although he was the most talented player on the team, he had enough of Coach Malone and basketball in general after this season.

As CJ's mom pulled into the driveway, he turned off his music and opened the car door. She looked at him in the rearview mirror and said, "Remember kiddo, there are no losses in life, just lessons."

Sydney Harding was an incredible mother who loved her children the way every child deserved to be loved, unconditionally. She was an attractive lady in her early forties with blondish hair and bright blue eyes. As a single mother, she somehow kept her youthful looks and was always full of life. She was a natural optimist who always looked on the bright side of everything. Lately, though, she was having trouble connecting with her son, and she was becoming concerned. The ninth grade had been really difficult for CJ. Although he had a decent basketball season, he was unmotivated, underachieving in the classroom, and lifeless at home.

Mrs. Harding looked back at her son, searching for the right thing to say. Thinking his favorite food may cheer him up, she asked, "How about pizza tonight, champ?" She was smart enough not to talk about the game.

She remembered going to her late husband's games in high school. They were the All-American couple. She was the cheer captain, and Chad was the star athlete. After the games, he would always say, "Let's not talk about the game. Coaches coach and fans cheer. Let's just enjoy this moment together." She remembered those words and never mentioned any specific things to CJ about basketball. That was for his coaches; her job was to support and encourage him unconditionally.

Mrs. Harding knew that it had been a challenging basketball season for CJ, yet she did not know exactly how to handle it. She did not have a lot of respect for Coach Malone, but she did not want to meddle too much. She had been around sports long enough to see pushy parents complaining about every little thing, so she decided to let CJ try to resolve any problems that might arise. As a single parent, she was mindful about raising self-reliant children.

CJ was in no mood to eat, and he ignored his mom's attempt to cheer him up. He sauntered up to his bedroom to listen to some more music. Mrs. Harding walked into the den where her eight-year-old daughter Katie and neighbor Tommy were playing X-box games with their babysitter. After paying the babysitter and walking her to the door, she sat down next to Katie and watched Tommy play his NBA video game. "How did the game go Mommy?" Katie asked.

"Not so well, kiddo," she replied in a matter of fact manner. "I'm afraid your brother is not going to be great company tonight."

"That's okay Mommy. Tommy and I will cheer him up." Katie had the positive energy of her mother. Like CJ though, she had the physical characteristics of her father, with big brown eyes and long eyelashes.

Mrs. Harding looked at her daughter admiringly and could not believe how much she had grown. Unfortunately, her late husband did not have a chance to meet the young dynamo.

"He would've been so proud of her," she thought to herself. Mrs. Harding discovered she was pregnant with Katie the same day she learned about the news of Chad's passing. It was such a roller coaster day, full of the highest of highs, and the lowest of lows.

She has yet to forget that fateful day, when two military officers stopped by her house. Hearing the doorbell, she ran to the door with young CJ in her arms and a spring in her step, bouncing from the news of her pregnancy. As she opened the door, her jaw dropped, knowing right away why the officers were there. Though they were polite, she could only say, "No," over and over again. She finally put CJ down and listened with disbelief as the officers told her that her husband had been killed in action while serving his country in Afghanistan. She cried, whispering to herself in disbelief, "No. Not Chad. Not now. How could this be?"

Mrs. Harding knew the cost of war. She had grieved with many wives in the past that had lost their husbands. Somehow, though, she thought she and Chad were different. Ever since she met Chad, he seemed to be destined for great things. He was so handsome, smart, and successful at everything he chose to do. He was such a good and decent person, never saying a bad word about anyone. Focused entirely on his future and the positive aspects of life, he simply did not have time for negativity. Sydney not only loved Chad, but he inspired her to become a better person. She truly believed that they would live happily ever after.

Suddenly, Mrs. Harding began to think about Tommy, who was busy running up the score of his NBA game on the Xbox. Tommy was an 11 year-old boy who always seemed to find his way over to the Harding's house. He had Asperger syndrome, a mild form of autism that affects thousands of young people. People diagnosed with this disorder often struggle in social situations, and their speech may sound different because of their inflection and tendency to repeat words.

Tommy took a special liking to CJ. He would always watch him shoot baskets in his backyard, and count the number of baskets he made. Tommy was a master at memorizing data, often reciting the stats of all his favorite NBA players to CJ and Katie, or anyone else who would listen. Mrs. Harding told Tommy it was time to leave, but not before he began to list all the statistics from his last Xbox game. As Tommy left, he shouted back towards the house, "Tell CJ I will count his shots tomorrow!"

CJ never came down for dinner that night and seemed to be in slow motion for the next few weeks. Mrs. Harding continued to worry about his attitude. The end of the basketball season had only exacerbated his somber mood. CJ did not play a spring sport for his school and also expressed to his mom that he no longer wanted to play on his AAU team. AAU or Amateur Athletic Union is a program that many serious basketball players competed in during the spring and summer. Although he was not the most motivated person, CJ had always loved basketball. But Mrs. Harding was afraid that, if he stopped playing, he would lose the one thing that truly made him happy. She also feared CJ would lose the only real connection he had with his father.

A graduate of West Rapids High, the same school in which CJ attended, CJ's late father was a three-star high school athlete and one of West Rapids' best basketball players of all time. He went on to play college basketball at West Point Academy for the legendary Coach Frank Taylor. His dad chose West Point because they had a great coach, but more importantly he had a strong desire to serve his country. West Point is an elite academy for future military officers and known for producing some of our country's greatest leaders.

Coach Taylor eventually moved on from the Academy and reached legendary status as one of the premier college coaches in the game. CJ could not watch sports news without seeing his dad's former coach on TV. He still remembered meeting him at a West Point reunion, where Coach Taylor had told him his dad was a true American hero and one of the best leaders that he had ever seen. For the first time ever, CJ realized what a legend his dad really was.

Looking back, Coach Taylor said something peculiar to CJ before he left. He said, "Your dad was a great player and a true champion. I look forward to finding out if his team was truly successful, and if I did a good job coaching them." CJ was too young and too shy to ask him what he meant, so he just turned his head and walked away.

CJ was a tall and handsome young man, who was very polite. Despite his height and good looks, he often felt unprepared and withdrawn in social situations and at school. He was shy around adults and quiet with his peers. He had friends, but he had never really connected with anyone. He also felt nervous around his teachers. Mostly, he was afraid of saying the wrong thing or making a mistake.

Because of his fear of failure, he would often just hang around, not involving himself in much of anything.

CJ could not go anywhere without someone mentioning his dad. His dad's presence was especially felt at West Rapids High. His state championship banner hung in the gymnasium's rafters, a big picture of him was framed in the All-State hallway, and a special memorial had been built in the front of the school, honoring him for his service to our country. There were even a few veteran teachers still around that had taught him. They often shared memories of his father with CJ, which he politely listened to, even though he had already heard the same stories dozens of times in the past.

The truth was CJ missed his dad, but the memories of him were gradually fading away every day. He barely remembered the funeral anymore, with all of the military officers, family, friends, and guns being shot over the casket. Sometimes, CJ would still wake up in the middle of the night hearing those haunting gun shots.

CJ's dad was buried at Arlington Cemetery in Washington, D.C. He had earned the prestigious Medal of Honor Award (the military's highest honor given for personal acts of bravery or going above and beyond the call of duty) and the Purple Heart (an award given to those in the military that were either wounded or killed in action) for his heroism. CJ could not remember all the details of his dad's death, but he knew that he saved many American lives from a terrorist ambush. CJ was secretly proud of his dad, but it was hard for him to live in the shadow of such a great man.

Chapter 1 Questions to Ponder:

- What was CJ's mindset when he was attempting the last shot of the game? How do you think that affected the outcome?
- What was CJ's relationship with Coach Malone? Have you ever had a coach or teacher like Coach Malone? Explain.
- Describe CJ's dad. How do you think his tragic death affected his family?
- Why do you think CJ has so much trouble living in his dad's shadow?

Chapter 2:

Compare and Despair

Mrs. Harding walked into CJ's bedroom with her daily morning wake up call, "Rise and shine! It's time for school!" CJ rolled over, with no motivation to get out of bed.

Katie was already eating breakfast at the kitchen island, preparing for the day. CJ eventually sauntered into the kitchen, bemoaning the fact that today was the end of the third quarter. He knew his grades would be emailed to his mother by 3 p.m. This was not his finest quarter, and he was expecting the worst.

On his way to school, CJ checked his Twitter account and noticed the West Rapids' varsity basketball coach, Frank Reese, had just announced his retirement. He liked Coach Reese a lot, and thought he was going to play for him next year. When his dad attended West Rapids, Coach Reese oversaw the JV program, so CJ felt that he had a connection with him. Coach Reese was old school, but fair.

CJ paused for a moment, wondering if Coach Malone might be the next varsity coach. He wanted anybody but him. CJ felt Coach Malone was too negative and believed that the program needed a fresh start.

CJ knew that coaching was very difficult, especially at the high school level. The West Rapids' parents were very demanding and involved in all of the athletic programs. He knew the next coach would not only need to be able to coach basketball but also handle all of the nosey parents who tried to influence the coaches and administrators.

That day, everyone at school was talking about the next coach. After all, West Rapids was a large school with an excellent athletic program. Even though the school had won only one state basketball championship; West Rapids was always very competitive and won many league titles. Not only was it a beautiful campus, it was also a great place to coach and teach.

Later that day, Coach Reese let the players know the school would be interviewing for the position in the next few weeks. He assured the team that they would hire an excellent coach that would continue the school's great basketball tradition.

CJ basically went through the motions in school and came home even more depressed than he had been. With the horrible ending to his JV season and the retirement of Coach Reese, he was seriously contemplating quitting basketball for good. He tended to think in negative terms and was almost certain that Coach Malone would be offered the job.

CJ had decided not to play AAU basketball during the spring, so he had a lot of time on his hands, most of which he spent shooting hoops in his backyard. Tommy eventually came outside and started counting his made shots. Tommy never bothered CJ; in fact, he liked his company. He felt Tommy liked him for who he was and never asked too much from him or compared him to anyone else.

As Mrs. Harding drove home from work, she thought about the conversation she was going to have with CJ about his report card. She was one of the best real estate agents in the area – a hard worker who was very good with people. Unfortunately, her job had unpredictable hours, so she relied on many of her neighbors and friends for help with her children. If the task of being a single parent was tough, no one would have ever known by speaking to her. She never complained and was very grateful for her children.

Sydney Harding's number one priority was raising her children. With her good looks and positive energy, most people in the community were surprised that she chose not to remarry or even date, for that matter. Many people assumed she was still devastated by the loss of her husband and too focused on raising her children. Others presumed she was not ready for another relationship. The deeper truth was that she did not have many opportunities to date. Many men were either intimidated by her looks and charm, or felt that she was way out of their league. Others were daunted by the legacy of her late husband. Everyone either knew Chad personally or knew of him. The idea of trying to replace him was unthinkable for most guys.

After picking up Katie from the latchkey program at her elementary school, Mrs. Harding pulled into their driveway. CJ, in an effort to avoid conversation with his mom, motioned to Tommy, and they immediately went inside. Mrs. Harding privately wondered why CJ did not excel in school. She had been a pretty good student, and Chad earned straight A's in high school and excelled at the Academy. In fact, during his senior year at West Point, he was ranked number one in his class and later received the Distinguished Graduate Award.

After graduation, he served his required years of service and later became the CEO of a small automobile supply company. Chad had offers to work for major corporations in New York and Chicago but turned them down to move back to his hometown with Sydney. They were living the American dream until that fateful day on September 11, 2001.

Life before September 11th seemed like a fairy tale to Mrs. Harding. She was married to the man of her dreams, and they had recently moved back to their hometown in western Michigan. They lived in a beautiful neighborhood, with family and friends all around.

Chad was a dreamer and would always talk about their future in such a positive way. He was able to make even the smallest moments precious and was so exhilarating to be around. He was a serious man with many responsibilities, but his number one priority was his family. He would spend countless hours reading, playing ball, or even singing with CJ.

Of all the accomplishments and awards Chad had earned in his life, his son brought him his greatest joy.

Unfortunately, after the terrorist attacks, everything changed. Chad felt a patriotic duty to serve his country, so he reenlisted in the Army. Mrs. Harding remembered the conversation like it was yesterday. Chad loved his family immensely but felt his country needed him. As Mrs. Harding reflected on the conversation, she thought, "That was so Chad. He always put others before himself." He always did the right thing, and he wanted to be a great example for his son. "Duty, Honor, and Country" were not just words in a mission statement at West Point; rather, they were words that Chad lived by.

Katie ran into the house with her usual enthusiasm, and Mrs. Harding followed her through the door, thinking about what she would say to CJ. She wanted to be firm but not crush his spirits. She felt he was in a bad place and did not want to make things worse by judging him. CJ was such a great kid, but his self-esteem was fragile. She knew this would be a difficult conversation, and she had to strike a balance between being supportive and being firm. She asked herself, "What would Chad say?"

CJ and Tommy were eating snacks in the kitchen, when his mom came into the room with a serious look on her face. CJ knew what was coming and put his head down, feeling both embarrassed and ashamed. He had trouble making eye contact with most adults in his life, not just his mother. CJ's posture was always slouched, giving him the appearance that he did not care much about anything.

Tommy, who had a difficult time picking up on social cues, started recalling CJ's made shots from the afternoon. He would list them from the left side of the hoop, and then from the right, momentarily boosting CJ's pride. Mrs. Harding, who never had difficulty speaking directly to Tommy, told him it was time to go home. CJ knew what was coming next.

In a caring, yet firm voice, Mrs. Harding began by saying, "I love you so much, CJ, and you are so smart. How can you get a report card like this? I just don't know what to do anymore."

She continued, "You mope around here all day either shooting hoops or playing video games. What's going on? One of your dad's favorite lines from West Point was, 'always choose the hard right over the easy wrong.' CJ, school is the hard right. You need to choose school."

CJ was already in a defensive mood but hearing another West Point quote and the mere mention of his dad put him over the top. "Well, Dad isn't here, is he?" he asked, raising his voice in anger.

He added, "I'm not Dad! Sorry, I'm not perfect. Sorry, I'm not an all 'A' student or West Point material. I guess I'm a big disappointment. I hate school, and I hate Dad too for not being here."

CJ rushed out of the kitchen and escaped to his bedroom, where he listened to more music. He thought about what a failure he was. He felt that he was a big disappointment to his family, to his teammates, and to his school.

CJ had a tendency to be very pessimistic, often using negative self-talk and thinking to himself, "I'm so stupid. I can't do anything right." He sat in his room more depressed than ever, thinking of his dad, assuming he was looking down at him with great disappointment. He wanted to move, get out of this community, and start all over, where nobody knew him, and most importantly, nobody knew his dad! CJ tweeted, "I hate school, want to transfer."

Chapter 2 Questions to Ponder

- Why do you think CJ was so nervous about his report card?
- Why do you think CJ became so defensive with his mother? How could he have handled it differently?
- Why do you think CJ's dad turned down high level jobs in New York and Chicago and decided to move back to his hometown?
- How did CJ feel at the end of the chapter? Have you ever felt like this? Explain.

Chapter 3

Finding Inspiration

CJ woke up late Saturday morning at 11:15 a.m. Katie was already outside swinging on the swings, enjoying a beautiful Michigan spring day, while Mrs. Harding was out in the garage moving some old boxes. CJ stared out of the kitchen window, looking at his mother and feeling guilty about his tirade last week. He had always been slow to apologize, but a few days had passed since the incident, and it was time to make amends. CJ had too much respect for his mother. She was an amazing woman, and the last thing he wanted to do was to be an extra burden for her. CJ went out to the garage, and in his own awkward way of apologizing, asked, "Do you need any help, Mom?"

She smiled and said, "Hey, sleepy. I was getting worried about you."

"I'm fine, Mom."

"You've been sleeping a lot. Maybe you're growing?" She was about to mention that his dad was 6'4", but caught herself and said, "Thanks for coming out. I need your strength with some of this old stuff. I am going through some of these boxes for the Salvation Army."

CJ took a heavy box and moved it to the center of the garage. He then started looking through all the boxes and could not believe how full they were. He noticed that many of the items belonged to his dad, including old clothes, random military items, and a lot of memorabilia.

CJ knew how much his mother loved his dad. Her face always lit up when people would tell stories about him. He started feeling more and more guilty about their argument.

CJ put his head down to avoid eye contact and in an apologetic tone, said, "Mom, you know I don't hate Dad. I was just frustrated, and I shouldn't have said what I said."

His mom looked at him affectionately and replied, "I know you don't, honey. He would be so proud of you. Your dad's face always lit up when he saw you. His favorite thing to do was come home and play with you. He would raise you up high and say, 'Together we can do great things.' He loved you so much, CJ."

"Really?" he questioned with interest.

"Oh yes," his mom continued. "Your dad always had quotes and sayings he learned from Coach Taylor or from West Point. In fact, I remember the first words he said to me after he asked me to marry him. He said the same thing to me that he would always say to you. 'Sydney, together we're going to do great things.' He was always so positive and motivating!"

CJ smiled at the story but felt deep down that his dad would not be that proud of him. After all, he was nowhere near the student his father was, and though he was pretty good at basketball, he was not close to playing college basketball. His dad just seemed to be larger than life.

CJ took another box from his mother and noticed it was full of books and binders. He asked, "What's all this stuff?"

"Oh, your dad was a big reader and owned a ton of books. Look through those bigger boxes and see what we can throw out."

Pulling out an old binder, he asked curiously, "What about this one, Mom?"

His mom looked at it closely and recalled, "Oh, your dad was working on a project but never had a chance to finish it. He wanted to write a manual that would be used to build elite officers in the military. Along with a business degree, your dad had a master's degree in psychology. He thought he could help the military with leadership training."

She added, "He also thought he could incorporate many of the lessons he learned from playing for the great Coach Taylor. Your dad loved that man and thought that if anyone could help America win the war in Afghanistan, it would be Coach Taylor."

CJ brushed the binder off and looked through it with great curiosity. It was hard to explain, but when holding the binder; he felt a special bond with his dad that he had never felt before. CJ looked up at his mom, who was climbing the ladder to reach a higher shelf, and asked, "Can I take this binder back to my room?"

She looked down and replied, "Of course, CJ. I'm not sure if your dad ever finished it, but I'm sure he would be happy for you to have it." With a newfound spring in his step, CJ walked back into the house and started reading the binder.

Chapter 3: Questions to Ponder

- Why do you think CJ finally apologized to his mother? Why is saying sorry so difficult?
- Why did CJ's dad write the manual?
- Why do you think CJ was so excited about the binder?
- What is psychology? How could CJ's dad's background in psychology help him with leadership training?

Chapter 4

Education

The binder contained handwritten notes that were neater than any he had ever seen before. He thought sarcastically to himself, "Go figure. My dad had perfect penmanship too." The beginning seemed to be a mission statement on why the country needs elite officers and leaders in the armed forces. The binder was full of bullet point notes, poetry, motivational quotes, and stories. His dad was an inspirational writer, and his words motivated CJ like no other words have before. He could not put it down.

His dad created an acronym for the word elite. Each section was divided up according to each letter. The letter "E" stood for *education*. His dad explained, "One cannot be elite without an education. An education does not mean what kind of grades you earn. A real education is a result of the energy and effort a person puts into being the best version of himself through his studies and curiosity."

With great interest, CJ started taking notes, reading that education is about having a mindset of success. He really enjoyed reading what his dad had to say about the brain, and how it can change. He read, "Our brain grows with every challenge, and the more challenges you take on, the more your brain will grow." He also learned about two features of the brain, neurons and myelin. "You start your life with around 100 billion neurons and your brain is like a big muscle, it gets stronger the harder you work it. Myelin helps you become a better student, athlete, leader, and thinker." The fact that, if challenged, myelin can grow every day, fascinated CJ. He continued to read, "Curiosity is a key ingredient to a solid education." CJ was a mediocre student in school, and he always thought he was nothing but a dumb jock. He had no idea that his brain could actually grow.

His dad's manual emphasized that elite officers value education over everything else. He wrote, "Knowledge is power." CJ continued to read about the importance of curiosity and effort. His dad also cited a study conducted by Stanford psychology professor Carol S. Dweck, Ph.D., about one's mindset. She discovered, after years of research, that people either have a fixed or a growth mindset.

A fixed mindset simply means your talent and smarts are fixed at birth and cannot be developed. People with a fixed mindset tend to avoid challenges and try not to look bad in front of others. On the other hand, if people have growth mindsets, their brains and talents are just the starting point, since improvement can be made through effort and hard work. His dad wrote, "Elite officers must have a growth mindset and then build that same mindset in their soldiers. All great leaders have a growth mindset and are not afraid to fail."

CJ reflected on his own mindset, believing he was too fixed minded. He did not like how his freshman basketball season ended. He was so afraid that he would miss the last shot, he froze on the court. CJ was beginning to understand that he had to become more growth minded. He also started to think that he had more control over his own destiny.

His dad also wrote that officers who sit in the front rows of military training tend to listen more and are less distracted. He continued, "Everything you do sends a message. Learn to listen and listen to learn. It is important to send the message to your instructors or your officers that learning is important, and you are very interested in self-improvement."

CJ really liked the next section about goal setting. His dad wrote, "Success is not random. Successful people have goals, and very successful people write their goals down." His dad also referenced a study overseen by Mark McCormack. Mr. McCormack interviewed students from an elite college and asked them, "Have you set clear, written goals for your future and made plans to accomplish them?" He found that 84 percent did not have any goals, 13 percent had goals but did not write them down, and only three percent of the students had written their goals down on paper.

The most interesting aspect of the study was that 10 years later, the same students from that elite college were interviewed again. CJ was fascinated to find out that the 13 percent of the class who had goals were earning, on average, twice as much as the 84 percent who had no goals. CJ was also amazed to learn about the three percent who had written their goals out on paper. They were earning, on average, 10 times as much as the other 97 percent of alumni combined.

His dad was hitting home the importance of writing down your goals on paper. CJ thought about his own future and began writing out the goals he personally wanted to accomplish.

He read throughout the afternoon, as well as the rest of the weekend, about the value of education and how it is the first principle of becoming an elite officer or person. CJ paid extra attention to a quote by Bob Moawad which read, "The best day of your life is the one in which you decide your life is your own. No apologies or excuses – no one to lean on, rely on, or blame. The gift is yours. It is an amazing journey and you alone are responsible for the quality of it. This is the day that your life really begins." CJ read this quote over and over again. He felt a sense of excitement about his future and the possibilities that were ahead of him. He couldn't wait for the fourth quarter marking period to begin.

On Monday morning, CJ's energy was so high that it rivaled his little sister Katie's. They sat and chatted through breakfast, and CJ was unusually excited about school. He looked at his mother and said with enthusiasm, "Hey, Mom. Did you know we are studying about the Civil War in Social Studies class? Many of the officers who fought in the war went to

West Point, just like Dad. General Lee, who fought for the Confederates, was ranked second in his class. Dad was first! He was smarter than all those great generals."

Mrs. Harding was stunned, yet also thrilled, to see CJ suddenly become so motivated. She had never heard CJ brag about his father or be that excited about his studies at school. She began to wonder just what Chad had written in that notebook.

"How smart was the guy who fought for the North?" Katie questioned.

CJ responded with a smile and, in a thoughtful manner, replied, "Well, General Grant, who also went to West Point, was ranked 21st out of 39 in his class. But what made him great was that he was not afraid to make mistakes, Katie. He was growth minded and aggressive. Great leaders are not afraid to make mistakes. Remember that, Katie."

CJ rushed out of the house ready to attack the school day with great enthusiasm and energy. Always one of the tallest kids in his classes, he had sat in the back of the classroom every year since first grade so that he would not obstruct anyone's view of the teacher. But today he asked every one of his teachers if he could sit in the front row. His teachers were very impressed. Though CJ was still shy and avoided eye contact, they appreciated his initiative and moved his seat to the front.

CJ took notes in each class and even asked a few questions, which was very unusual for him. His dad's motivational words about the importance of education and curiosity were really making a difference. Mostly though, he wanted to grow his brain's myelin. This was the first time in his life that CJ thought he could get smarter every day.

During school announcements, CJ heard that the new varsity basketball coach was going to have a meeting at lunch time. He overheard some of the varsity players saying that it wasn't Coach Malone, but, rather, a man named Charlie Dailey, an alumnus of the school who had previously coached a smaller high school to the regional finals. He was also the son of a former Division I coach from the area. Word quickly traveled around school that he was a players' coach who liked to play an up-tempo game. In addition, he was the last player from West Rapids High to play Division I college basketball.

CJ walked into the basketball meeting a few minutes late and had to sit near the back. Right away, he thought he was making a bad first impression. "I should be sitting in the front," he thought to himself as he listened to the new coach.

Coach Dailey gave an impressive talk, and the players seemed excited about the future of West Rapids basketball. Afterwards, they lined up and introduced themselves. CJ was last in line. When it was his turn, he glanced down, gave a weak handshake and introduced himself as CJ Harding. Coach Dailey enthusiastically shook his hand and asked, "Are you related to the famous Chad Harding?"

CJ looked up, and with some newfound confidence, proudly smiled and replied, "Yeah. He was my father."

Coach Dailey responded, "Well, he was my favorite player when I was growing up. My dad recruited him, and he took me to a lot of your dad's games. He was a big inspiration. It is an honor to meet you, young man. I expect great things from you."

"Thanks, coach. I really appreciate it," CJ replied with a half-smile. This was the first time in a long while that CJ had not been turned off by someone complimenting his dad. In fact, it made him feel pretty good. It also reminded him that he needed to go home and finish his homework. He wanted to continue to grow his brain.

After CJ completed all of his homework, he set specific goals for himself. He wanted to take 500 shots a day, improve upon the timing of his mile run, and increase his strength through sit-ups and push-ups. He remembered that his dad wrote how important it was to write down goals and be committed to them every day. So, CJ decided to write his goals down on note cards and place them on his bedside table.

He thought to himself, "Who is going to hold me accountable to these goals? Who can I ask to help me stay motivated?" CJ smiled when he realized who would be the perfect person. He went over to Tommy's house and explained his plan to him. Tommy was excited to help, and he would be ready to shoot and workout every day.

Their workout plan consisted of Tommy recording every shot CJ made. Tommy would also time CJ's mile run with a stopwatch, and record results as CJ skipped rope and completed push-ups. Tommy's mother walked out of the house with a curious look on her face. She had always appreciated the relationship CJ had with Tommy. Raising a child with Asperger's was difficult, so she felt very blessed to live next door to such a wonderful family like the Hardings. Together, Mrs. Harding and Katie walked outside to see what Tommy and CJ were doing. The three of them stood at the backyard fence and watched with amazement. It was truly a sight to see.

After his workout and homework were completed, CJ had plenty of time to read his dad's manual. He went to his bedroom and wrote the word **ELITE** on a white note card. He taped it on his bedside table next to his goals, where he could see them every day. There was still a lot left to read from his dad's notebook, and he could not wait to continue growing myelin.

CJ picked up the manual and reviewed all of his dad's major points on education. He was feeling motivated for the first time in his life. CJ also noticed that simple things like being more curious about learning and sitting in the front row had really made a positive impact on his performance at school.

Mrs. Harding was very impressed by CJ's recent transformation. However, when she saw his report card, she was utterly amazed. CJ had earned all A's for the fourth quarter marking period. Although, CJ was happy with his improvement, he was not yet entirely satisfied.

With the upcoming summer quickly approaching, he established two new goals for himself: to continue his basketball training with Tommy and read five books before the next school year began. CJ knew his dad was a big reader, and he wanted to read as much as he could. His newfound knowledge about the brain encouraged him to continue to learn. CJ was going to be a sophomore next year, and he wanted to build upon his recent successes and continue to improve.

Chapter 4: Thoughts to Ponder

- What is the difference between having a fixed mindset and a growth mindset?
- Why are goals so important? Do you have goals? Are they written down? Why do you think people who write down their goals are much more successful?
- What is Asperger's? Why is Tommy's mom so grateful that she and Tommy live next to the Hardings? How do you treat others that might be different from you?
- What is myelin and how do you grow it?
- How exactly did CJ improve his performance at school? What are you doing to improve your own performance at school?

Chapter 5
Leadership

Over the summer, CJ continued to read his dad's manual.   Even though the notebook was very detailed, he could tell his dad did not have an opportunity to finish it.   CJ summarized all of the major points on education, and it was finally time to go on to the next section.   The second letter in the word **ELITE** stood for *leadership*.

CJ's father had played for one of the greatest college basketball coaches of all time, was ranked number one in his class at West Point, was the CEO of a successful company, and was a leader of men on the battlefield.   From these experiences, he certainly had a lot of insights on leadership.   CJ read, "Elite people yearn for leadership, and leadership is a choice, not a position.   True leaders have a vision and the ability to communicate that vision to other people.   Leaders do not take days off.   They are confident, without being arrogant.   The world is run by confident people."

CJ was motivated by his father's words. He began to take notes and highlight specific points, particularly focusing on what his dad had written about transformational leaders. "There are transitional leaders and transformational leaders. Transitional leaders simply lead their team through one activity to the next with very basic goals ahead of them. Transformational leaders make a difference in the lives of those they lead. They make those around them better. They are so excited about their vision that they bring others with them." CJ was very excited, as he imagined himself becoming a transformational leader, not only on the basketball court, but also in the classroom.

CJ's father also included a story about a famous French prince written by Sean Covey. King Louis XVI was dethroned, and his son was kidnapped. The kidnappers did not want to kill the young prince and make him a martyr, but they thought that if they could destroy the young man's mindset, he would never be fit to be a king. They took the prince away and exposed him to evil things, while also promising him riches and a life of luxury if he would denounce his father. They surrounded him with everything that could destroy a young man, but the prince would not waver. Finally, after six months of captivity, his kidnappers asked him why he was so loyal to France and to his father. The prince looked at them and said, with great confidence, "I cannot partake in the things you ask, for I was born to be a king."

His dad explained that elite leaders need to have the same discipline and mindset as the young prince did in Covey's story. Like the prince, leaders need to have a strong vision of their destiny. He wrote, "Elite leaders should be too disciplined to partake in activities that would derail them." CJ thought a lot about the story and reflected on all the bad decisions that he had made over the past few years. He started to develop a more positive vision for his life, focusing on the goals he was committed to and the decisions that would help him become the best that he could be.

CJ kept reading throughout the summer months. He took notes and reread different bullet points and poems. He also read all about the importance of body language, eye contact, and a firm handshake. His dad wrote, "Elite leaders are great communicators. Fifty-five percent of how we communicate is with our body language, 38 percent of how we communicate is with our tone of voice, and only seven percent is with the words we say."

CJ reflected on his own poor posture and meek voice. He felt that he did not walk or sound like a leader should. After reading his father's words on leadership, he was determined to look, sound, and act like a person destined for greatness. CJ took time to visualize what confident body language and tone of voice would look and sound like in different social settings.

CJ had one of the best summers of his life. He and Tommy continued to work out every day. He also read a ton of great books, including the required summer reading list for school. For the very first time in his life, CJ felt a special connection to his dad. He even started asking his mom more questions about him.

One rainy summer day he approached her in the kitchen. "Mom, what was Dad's favorite book?"

Mrs. Harding perked up, as she loved talking about Chad. She looked at CJ with a smile and said, "Oh, your dad loved all kinds of books. He read leadership books and biographies all the time. He loved finding out what separated the great people from average people. He especially liked reading about West Point leaders and basketball coaches."

CJ listened intently and maintained great eye contact. His mom continued by saying, "Yet I did see him reading a lot of fiction too. He enjoyed a good story and learned a lot from the various conflicts that the fictional characters endured. Your dad was a big believer in emotional intelligence. He felt that the most important quality for successful people was their ability to relate to other people."

She added, "Your dad believed reading rich literature helped increase one's ability to lead others. His favorite book of all time was *To Kill a Mockingbird*, and his favorite character was Atticus Finch. Your dad thought that Atticus was the best father, who always chose the hard right over the easy wrong."

CJ remembered reading *To Kill a Mockingbird* last summer and not really enjoying it. In fact, he thought it was boring. Ironically, the book was still on his bookshelf in his bedroom. He thanked his mom and rushed into his room to find it. CJ read the book enthusiastically and understood the storyline much better this time, learning a lot from Atticus Finch.

The summer seemed to fly by, and CJ couldn't believe the first day of school was already near. He was really excited about beginning his sophomore year of high school. Tommy was now in the 7th grade. Since the junior high campus was annexed to the high school, Tommy and CJ would be driving to school together every day. CJ did not mind carpooling since he and Tommy had become pretty close over the summer. Tommy was quirky for sure, but he seemed like he was part of the family. CJ felt very comfortable around him.

CJ had a great first day of school. He carried himself much differently than he had in the past. He remembered his dad's major points on leadership and body language. CJ recalled his dad writing, "Everything you do sends a message."

With a firm handshake, CJ introduced himself to his teachers. He looked them in the eyes and expressed that their classes were important to him. He also asked each teacher if he could sit in the front of the classroom. All of his teachers agreed and were impressed with CJ, as he seemed so focused and excited for their classes.

As the first day of school came to an end, CJ saw Tommy at a distance waiting for him to walk home.

Two senior basketball players named Derek and Stan were walking by Tommy. A little nervous and out of his comfort zone, he began to mumble and repeat himself in an awkward manner. Tommy's Asperger's was not really understood by many of the students.

Stan, who was a nice enough guy, was the lone returning starter from the team. Though nice, he was not socially confident. He tended to emulate whatever his peers did. Derek, meanwhile, was a reserve on the team last year and was hoping to start this upcoming season. He had a good shot, but his short stature limited him. Some people thought the only reason Derek received playing time last season was because his dad would often call Coach Reese and complain. Derek's family was wealthy, and they tried to influence whomever they could.

Derek looked at Tommy and said in a demeaning tone, "You got a problem there, kid." Stan just nervously laughed along with Derek. Tommy blushed and stuttered more, and Derek just laughed and said, "You are one weird dude."

As they left, Derek brushed Tommy and knocked him off balance. CJ walked closer to Tommy but chose not to say anything to Derek or Stan. CJ put his head down to avoid conflict and started walking home with Tommy. CJ felt bad for Tommy, but he was uncomfortable around Derek and Stan. He thought it would be best not to say anything. It was a quiet walk home.

Privately, CJ was conflicted about the incident between Derek and Tommy. CJ knew Derek was a bully, but he did not know how to handle the situation. West Rapids was a great school, but bullying was a major issue. It could range from seniors playing typical pranks on the younger students like stealing their lunches or mocking them, or the jocks walking around school like they owned the place. Over the last couple of years, cyber-bullying had also increased. One girl from CJ's middle school transferred to another school after a group of "mean" girls created a fake Facebook page that mocked her and featured disparaging rumors about her. CJ couldn't understand how people could be so mean to one another.

The incident was soon forgotten, and CJ and Tommy stayed committed to their workout plan. CJ would do his homework, and at 5 p.m. sharp, they would begin their training routines. Tommy would track CJ's improvement in shots made, as well as the mile run. CJ was amazed at Tommy's memory and dedication to helping him become the best he could be. CJ did not know a lot about Asperger's but could tell that Tommy had trouble in social situations and felt bad for him. His mom always told him, "Everyone has a story, CJ. If you take time to learn their story, it's easier to like them." CJ liked Tommy a lot. At the end of their session, he gave him a high five.

With his head down, Tommy said, "Thanks for being my friend, CJ."

CJ smiled and said, "You are a great teammate, Tommy. Don't let those guys at school bother you. Nobody likes them anyway." Tommy walked back to his house, smiling proudly.

After dinner, CJ continued reading more of his dad's notes concerning the topic of leadership. He started feeling worse about the situation with Tommy and Derek. He reflected on the different characters from the books he had read this past summer, especially Atticus Finch from *To Kill a Mockingbird*.

Atticus was so strong and seemed to be very self-confident. CJ felt that he should have stood up for Tommy. Instead, he chose the "easy wrong" by ignoring the situation. CJ knew that if he wanted to be a leader, he would need to have more courage in social situations and be committed to living according to the West Point creed, "Always choose the hard right over the easy wrong."

As CJ continued to read about leadership, he highlighted and took detailed notes on the manual's section about vision and imagination. "Leaders have a vision for their life and a creative imagination to accomplish their dreams." He also read about visualization, remembering his dad had written that the brain cannot tell the difference between a real event and an imagined event. If CJ could visualize success, his brain would start to rewire. All evening, he imagined himself answering questions in class, making the last second free throw on the basketball court, and even making the right decisions in social situations.

CJ received all A's on his first quarter report card and was becoming more confident in school and around his friends. He was excited for basketball season to begin. He had been the leading scorer on the junior varsity team last season, and this year he was most likely going to start on the varsity team, which many believed was in a rebuilding stage. CJ's dedication to becoming an elite person was really making a difference. Not only was he excelling in school, but he had transformed his physique too. He was bigger, stronger, and faster. He looked really good in the open gyms leading up to the tryouts.

CJ was also building a good relationship with Coach Dailey. Remembering his dad's words, "Seek mentors in life," CJ sought Coach Dailey's advice and really liked him as a person. At 33 years of age, Coach Dailey still looked like he was in playing shape. He was smart, funny, and had a passion for leadership. Like CJ's dad, he studied psychology in college and knew how to motivate. Unlike Coach Malone, he was also a big believer in using positive reinforcement to motivate his players.

When it came to coaching, Coach Dailey had a great pedigree. His dad was a local college coach at a small Division I school where he won over 500 games and was inducted into the Michigan Basketball Coaches Association Hall of Fame. He was also a great mentor who had taught Coach Dailey not only about basketball, but about life as well. He believed that basketball was a great vehicle to teach life lessons, from how to have a great attitude to being committed to excellence in all that you do. He also stressed putting others' needs ahead of your own. His two favorite plays in basketball were to assist on offense and to take a charge on defense, each of which symbolized unselfish play. To successfully execute each play, individual players must have a team first mentality.

Ironically, Coach Dailey's father recruited Chad Harding to play college basketball for him. He would often tell people, "He was the one recruit who got away." He would also take Coach Dailey to see Chad play and explain, "This kid plays basketball the right way." Coach Dailey knew a lot about basketball, not only from listening to his dad but also by watching Chad Harding play in high school. He learned early on how basketball was meant to be played.

Once the varsity team was selected, CJ was excited for the season to finally begin. His overall improvement on the basketball court was obvious. CJ was by far the best player on the team. The seniors were all hard workers and complemented each other extremely well. The one noticeable change was the addition of a transfer student named Carl Bozeman, who had recently moved in from the southeastern part of the state. He was an African-American guard who was lightning quick and could see the court extremely well. Carl was a nice young man who fit in really well with the team. CJ and Carl instantly became friends. Carl was impressed with how mature and driven CJ was, while CJ liked how laid back and confident Carl was. With the improvement of CJ and the addition of Carl, Coach Dailey began to wonder whether a supposed rebuilding year, may actually become a championship season.

CJ continued to maintain an A average and, as a result, was becoming more noticed in school. His teachers and peers were very impressed with his leadership ability and his commitment in the classroom. School administrators began to seek CJ out to help them organize school events. Kids in his class were also starting to ask him to hang out. All of a sudden, his followers on Twitter jumped from 110 to over 500.

The season started out very well as the Knights enjoyed a 4-1 record prior to the Christmas holiday. CJ was the team's leading scorer, while Carl was even better than people originally thought. His playmaking ability was remarkable. Carl was one of those players who simply made everyone on the court better.

Coach Dailey made sure that everyone on the team worked hard and was well prepared for each game. The only issue thus far was team chemistry. The players liked each other, but they did not really trust each other. The seniors did not like the attention that CJ and Carl were attracting, and they were becoming resentful. They would make comments here and there like, "Coaches' pet" or sarcastically say, "Here comes the super sophomore."

Coach Dailey, who occasionally witnessed the disparaging comments, chose to ignore the situation, hoping they would eventually stop.

Chapter 5: Thoughts to Ponder

- What did CJ learn about leadership?
- What did CJ learn about body language? Why do you think body language is so important when you communicate with others?
- What is the difference between transitional leadership and transformational leadership? Do you know any transformational leaders? Explain.
- What does it mean to choose the "hard right over the easy wrong"? Reflect on the most difficult decision you have ever had to make.
- Do you know kids like Stan and Derek? Why do you think people treat others badly?
- Describe Coach Dailey. Do you think he has a chance to be a great coach? What were some characteristics of some great teachers or coaches that you have had? Why do you think he chose to ignore some bad behaviors from his team? Do you think this was a good idea?

Chapter 6

Integrity

Mrs. Harding loved the holiday season; it was her favorite time of year. Family was very important to her. The first few Christmases without her husband had been incredibly tough, but she learned to focus on her kids and cherished the extra time that she had with them. The house was decorated beautifully, and Katie's boundless energy made the Christmas season even more special. CJ used the extra time to read more of his dad's notes on the meaning of the word elite. Currently serving as the president of his class and involved in different after school clubs, CJ was beginning to understand the importance of education and leadership. The more CJ became involved in extra-curricular activities, the more he enjoyed school. He remembered his dad's words about involvement and participation: "The more you put into something, the more you get out of it. Who you become is more important than what you do."

CJ reflected on who he wanted to become and how he wanted to lead. Most of the stories that he heard about his dad were focused on his great leadership and high character. CJ felt he was a leader by example through his hard work and dedication, but he was not quite sure how to be a vocal leader to a senior class who was obviously jealous of him.

CJ continued reading through his dad's notes and found that the "I" in elite stood for **integrity**. His dad wrote, "Integrity is when there is no gap between what you say and what you do." CJ looked at all of the notes, poems, and motivational quotes and continued to read his dad's words. "Integrity means doing the right thing, even when people are not looking. Integrity means you will never lie, cheat, or steal. One should be more concerned about his character than his reputation. Your reputation is what people think you are; your character is what you truly are." CJ also noticed a poem written by the renowned poet, Rudyard Kipling. As he read the poem, he especially liked the last stanza.

"If"

If you can talk with crowds and keep your virtue,
Or walk with kings - nor lose the common touch,
If neither foes nor loving friends can hurt you:
If all men count with you, but none too much;
If you can fill the unforgiving minute
With sixty seconds' worth of distance run,
Yours is the Earth and everything that's in it,
And - which is more - you'll be a Man, my son!

As he continued to read, he noticed another poem written by Peter Dale Wimbrow Sr. He really enjoyed this poem too; especially the first two stanzas.

When you get what you want in your struggle for
self
And the world makes you king for a day
Just go to the mirror and look at yourself
And see what that guy has to say.

For it isn't your father, or mother, or wife
Whose judgment upon you must pass
The fellow whose verdict counts most in your life
Is the one staring back from the glass.

CJ thought his dad included these two poems just for him. He occasionally felt uncomfortable around adults as well as some of the kids at school; especially the seniors. He was constantly worried about what others thought of him. These poems reminded him of the importance of just being your best self and not worrying about what other people thought.

CJ knew that his increased interest in education was preparing him to reach his goals. He also felt he was becoming a better communicator and leader. Nevertheless, he knew he had to step it up. He needed to be a young man of integrity who was comfortable in his own skin.

CJ recalled the prince in Sean Covey's story and on what integrity truly meant. He reflected on the first day of school when Tommy was being bullied and he did nothing. He also thought of all the times when he said bad things about other people behind their backs, as well as the negative comments he would often tweet. He never wrote anything really bad, but he wanted to be an elite athlete, someone who would be recruited by the best colleges in the country.

CJ remembered Coach Dailey telling the team, "College coaches talk to recruits' high school coaches, speak to their teachers, and even look on social media to find out anything negative." CJ looked through his tweets, amazed at how negative some of his comments were. He deleted everything that did not promote him in a positive way and made a commitment to tweet only optimistic messages. As he did, he also remembered a quote from his dad's notes: "There comes a time when you have to give up who you are, to become the person you want to be."

CJ continued to have a great basketball season and enjoyed playing with Carl immensely. They had great chemistry together. Carl was great off the dribble, while CJ had one of the sweetest shots anyone had ever seen. CJ's outstanding play was noticed not only at school, but by the loyal fan base as well. A group of older alumni, who came to every home game, started commenting on the similarities between the late Chad Harding and his son.

Now that Tommy was in middle school, he attended all of CJ's basketball games. He was his biggest fan and would amazingly remember all of his stats from each game. His memory was incredible. Mrs.

Harding, Katie, and CJ would often smile after games during their car rides home as Tommy provided all of the stats for each game.

Only one week was left of the regular season, and the Knights had a big game on Friday night against their cross-town rival Rockwood. This game was not only a neighborhood battle, but it would determine the league champion.

At Tuesday's practice, Coach Dailey did not seem himself. Practice was well organized as usual, but he looked distracted. CJ and Carl stayed after practice and each shot 100 free throws. They discussed how cool it would be to win a league championship together. CJ, remembering the importance of dreaming big said, "First a league championship, then a state championship."

Carl smiled as they walked off the court together. On their way out, they noticed Derek's dad, the school athletic director, and the school principal walking out of Coach Dailey's office. Derek's dad looked upset and continued talking to the administrators as they left the gymnasium.

"That explains what was up with Coach today," CJ said as they both looked at each other.

"Yeah. Looks like Derek's dad is not happy with his son's playing time," Carl replied with a sarcastic smile.

Throughout the season, Derek had been receiving less and less playing time. The truth of the matter was, the younger classmen were outplaying him. Coach Dailey could not afford to take CJ or Carl out of the game for any length of time, and there were just not enough minutes for Derek.

Derek's dad had a reputation of being a complainer, and he always tried to use his influence to get his way. He was an arrogant man who everyone pretended to like, but nobody respected. He thought he was better than everyone else.

Derek had many of his dad's personality traits, and he was not a very good teammate. He would always blame someone else when he would make a mistake or would have an excuse when something went wrong. CJ thought Derek was very fixed minded and a bully. He could not wait until he graduated.

To prepare for the championship game, the school organized a pep rally on Friday for the team during fourth hour. Junior high classes were invited to help build excitement, in hopes for a big turnout that night. Coach Dailey spoke to the students and introduced the players. He was an inspirational speaker, and the students cheered as he announced the team. However, CJ received the loudest cheers. Even though he was just a sophomore, he was the team's leading scorer and was becoming one of the more popular kids in school. His body language and demeanor exuded confidence, and he never said a bad word about anyone. Both the faculty and students respected him immensely.

When the crowd started chanting CJ's name, each of his teammates cheered, except for Derek. He rolled his eyes and whispered to Stan, "He is just a ball hog. He would be nothing without us." Stan just laughed and nodded his head approvingly while pretending to clap. As the team headed back to the locker room, Tommy, who was seated in the bleachers next to the locker room entrance, shouted in a nervous manner, "Hey, CJ. Good luck." CJ looked up and acknowledged Tommy.

He then saw Derek yell up into the bleachers in Tommy's direction, "Sit down you freak!" CJ looked back and saw most of the team laughing at Tommy, and he finally had enough.

Once they arrived in the locker room, CJ approached Derek quickly and said, "Hey, Derek. Why don't you pick on someone who can fight back? Your dad isn't here to fight your battles for you." Stan jumped in and held CJ back as Derek cowered. "That's what I thought, all talk. Really impressed you can pick on little kids. You're a piece of work." CJ turned around and left the locker room.

"You think you're real special," Derek shouted, suddenly finding his courage. "Nobody likes you on this team anyway." Just then, Coach Dailey came in and everyone dispersed. This was not the kind of team chemistry that Coach Dailey wanted just before the big game.

Later that evening, the gym was packed for the divisional championship game. Coach Dailey discussed his keys to success and then repeated the same three goals he mentioned before every game, "Play hard, play smart, and have fun." The team put their hands together and screamed, "Team!"

The game was close throughout the first half. CJ and Carl executed the pick and pop play extraordinarily well. CJ had four three-pointers during the first half, and the score was deadlocked at halftime.

As the team gathered in the locker room for their halftime adjustments, the players started grumbling at each other. Derek shouted, "Come on, guys. This is not a one man team!"

Stan followed by yelling, "We have to share the ball!"

CJ knew these remarks were directed at him and replied, "How about some other guys step up and do something?"

Coach Dailey quieted his players down by simply outlining his plan for the second half. He chose to ignore the negative comments. CJ liked how positive Coach Dailey was, but wished he was stronger and handled discipline issues better. The body language of the players was terrible, but Coach Dailey kept talking, hoping they could figure everything out during the second half.

The third quarter was a disaster. The West Rapids Knights were simply outplayed. They did not seem to trust one another, and the seniors had some selfish plays as well. Once they fell behind, they could not catch up, and they ended up losing an emotional game at home.

Coach Dailey tried to remain positive after the game, but everyone knew the team was falling apart. They tried to regroup as they prepared for the state tournament, but the team's chemistry was awful, and the players practiced like they were just going through the motions.

During the state tournament West Rapids won the first two district games against inferior opponents but lost in the district finals game, again to Rockwood High School. It was a real disappointing ending for CJ. Ironically, many of the players were happy when the basketball season ended. The seniors were tired of playing behind the underclassmen, and the underclassmen had enough of the bullying and obnoxious behavior from the seniors.

Although Coach Dailey was proud of their record, he was disappointed that his team did not reach its full potential, by losing two big games at the end of the season. He thought the team was selfish at times and regretted that he was not more proactive in his coaching. Privately, he mostly regretted backing down to Derek's dad. He felt that he played Derek more than he deserved because of the pressure he was feeling. He promised himself that he would coach his way in the future, no matter what anyone else said.

CJ was disappointed as they were driving home from their last game. He knew his team could have played better. Tommy let everyone in the car know CJ's statistics for the season. "You averaged 15.6 points per game, nine rebounds, six assists, shot 82 percent from the foul line, 42 percent from the three-point line, had 61 steals, took 16 charges, and had 24 blocked shots."

"Okay," CJ interrupted, "I appreciate the support. I'm going to take a few days off, and then we are back to training for next season. Right, Tommy?"

"I can't wait," Tommy responded.

As they pulled into the driveway, CJ tweeted out to his growing number of followers, "Tough loss tonight, stay positive. Can't wait until next year! #workhard #integrity."

CJ reflected a lot on the word integrity and reread some of his dad's quotes and poems. He felt he was still missing something, thinking to himself, "What could I have done differently? How can I be a young man of integrity? Where did my dad get so much of his strength from?"

Chapter 6: Thoughts to Ponder:

- What are CJ dad's thoughts on integrity? Why is integrity so important to leaders?
- Why do you think CJ was able to stand up to Derek this time around?
- Reread the stanza of the poem "If." What is the central message the author is conveying?
- What do you think about Derek's dad? Do some parents involve themselves too much in their children's sporting activities? Explain.
- What do you think were some contributing factors to West Rapids losing two big games at the end of the season? Explain.
- Why was Coach Dailey upset at the end of the season? What was his biggest regret?

Chapter 7

Team

CJ later found out that he had earned All-League, All County, and honorable mention All-State honors for his sophomore season. He was proud of his accomplishments, but he wanted more. He wanted to be elite. He wanted to be the best version of himself. So, CJ decided to continue his routine of finishing homework after school and then training with Tommy at 5 p.m.

He also continued to read his dad's notebook. The notes were sometimes hard to read because they were out of order. He was still able to find the section concerning the next letter in **ELITE** –"T" which stood for *team*. His dad wrote, "An elite person understands that he never makes it alone. He thinks of others before himself. Whether a neighbor, a classmate, a teammate, or a stranger, God puts people in our lives for different reasons, and we must bring as many people on our team as we can."

His father wrote repeatedly, "Team, Team, Team," throughout his notes. He also included poems and quotes that CJ read and reread. He especially liked a quote from Bob Moawad: "You can work miracles by having faith in others. By choosing to believe the best about people, you are able to bring out the best in them."

CJ started to think not only about his basketball team, but about his family as well. He reflected on his father's message and looked inward. He was particularly interested in his dad's quote about God putting people in his life for a reason and asked himself, "Who are the people in my life? How can I be a better teammate? How can I be a better classmate? How can I be a better friend? How can I be a better brother? How can I be a better son?" CJ was beginning to understand that being elite meant more than doing your best; it also meant bringing out the best in others.

Mrs. Harding woke CJ up on Monday morning with her "rise and shine" greeting, and he jumped out of bed ready to go. Knowing that elite athletes start the day with a great breakfast, CJ made himself some eggs and bacon. Thinking about his father's words, he knew that the word "team" meant more than people in a military unit or on a sports' team. He now understood that the teammates in your life also include your family.

CJ took time to ask Katie if she wanted some eggs and bacon. He then asked her what she was doing in school today. He was a good big brother, but this was the first time he really took a genuine interest in what his little sister was doing. She told him about all of the projects they were working on in class, and that she was really excited about her gymnastics recital on Friday night. As Mrs. Harding sipped her coffee, she looked at the two of them glowingly. CJ high-fived his sister and gave his mom a big kiss, and like a man on a mission rushed out the back door to go to school.

CJ texted Carl to meet up with him before first hour started. Carl approached him before the bell and asked, "What's up?"

CJ responded enthusiastically, "How about you and I work out together at five o'clock at my house after school today?"

"I'm in," Carl replied.

"Great. See you then. I cannot wait to introduce you to my trainer."

"You have a trainer?" Carl questioned in a confused tone. CJ walked away smiling.

After school, CJ had some chemistry homework to complete. He finished in plenty of time and went outside to wait for Tommy and Carl. Tommy saw CJ shooting from his window and came outside. CJ mentioned to him, "Look, you are so good at coaching me that I invited a teammate to come over to join us."

"Cool! Who is it?" Tommy asked.

"Carl," CJ replied.

"Oh, number 14, who averaged 10.6 points and 5.1 assists per game," Tommy replied. CJ just smiled and took a few shots while waiting for Carl. Carl showed up with Anthony, a 6'6" freshman who was the best player on the junior varsity team. He was talented enough to be on the varsity team but was too skinny to compete at the varsity level last season. He definitely had a lot of upside. The three of them took over 500 shots and then went on their mile run. When they came back, they each did 200 push-ups and skipped rope for two minutes. Tommy timed and counted everything. They split up the drills like station work; one would practice ball handling and dribbling exercises for five minutes, while the other two would shoot and rebound for each other. It was like a basketball clinic. CJ was complimenting and challenging his teammates. He was excited about the future of his team, remembering his dad's words, "Nobody makes it alone."

The boys followed the same routine every day and truly enjoyed hanging out together, as their camaraderie made the workouts more enjoyable. They had great chemistry. They even talked about inviting more kids to join them. They didn't want to leave anyone out. After their workout ended on Friday, Carl mentioned to Anthony and CJ that there was a big party over at Boulan Park and wondered if they were interested in going with him. Anthony jumped at the chance and said jokingly, "I'm in! A freshman hanging with two popular guys like the two of you? This will raise my profile."

CJ laughed but said, "Sorry, boys. I need to decline. I'm going to my sister's gymnastics recital tonight. I told her I would go."

Carl smiled and said, "That's cool. You're not only a great teammate, but a great brother too. Katie is very lucky."

CJ waved goodbye and went into his house to eat, shower, and get ready for the recital. In the shower, he reflected on the changes he had made in his life thus far. His focus on education, his commitment to leadership, his integrity, and the responsibility of being a great teammate on and off the basketball court had really changed his life.

After the recital, CJ took Katie out for ice cream. Considering CJ's busy schedule, it was difficult for the two of them to spend quality time together. He remembered his dad's words about teamwork and building relationships: "Teamwork is all about relationships. Relationships are the most important thing in any family, military unit, or team. Spend time to build great relationships in your life."

CJ complimented Katie on a brilliant performance. They had a great time together. He told Katie how proud he was to be her brother and that, if she ever needed anything, he would always be there for her. Judging from her body language, he could tell that she was having a lot of fun. As the two of them laughed throughout the evening, he remembered just how funny she could be. CJ was very proud of his choice to attend his sister's recital. He truly valued his relationship with his sister and was grateful that she was in his life. When they arrived home, he went straight to his room. He couldn't wait to finish reading his father's notes on teamwork.

CJ was especially interested in what his dad wrote about leaving a legacy. He read, "There are all kinds of different teams – good, bad, and, sometimes, great teams. But then, once in a while, there comes a group of individuals who are committed to a cause greater than their self-interests. They work, sacrifice, and dream together, but mostly they care about one another. These are the teams that have a chance to leave a legacy, to be remembered for doing something special, and make an impact on those around them." CJ wanted to be a leader on a legacy team and to positively impact his school and his family, just like his dad had.

As expected, the spring workouts were very successful. They even picked up a few more players. Each teammate challenged one another every day and held each other accountable for the goals they had written down.

They also decided to compete together in some competitive summertime AAU tournaments. Although most AAU teams are a collection of talented players throughout the state, they thought it would help them more if they just played together. As long as Coach Dailey did not coach them and the younger players volunteered to play in the older division, it was legal to do. Anthony's dad volunteered to coach and, of course, Tommy was a member of the team as its student manager and assistant coach.

Chapter 7: Thoughts to Ponder

- Why do you think it was important for CJ to reach out to Carl and his other teammates and invite them to train with them?
- Describe how CJ's relationship with Katie improved. How can you improve your relationships with your siblings, cousins, or friends?
- Have you ever been on a team that did not get along? What were the major issues? Did they prevent your team from becoming the best that it could be? Explain.
- What is a legacy team? Have you ever been a member of one? Explain.

Chapter 8

Excellence

CJ and his teammates played in a couple of AAU tournaments against some of the top college recruits in the area. Although they were improving, they lost most of their games. CJ was becoming increasingly impatient. He could not understand why he was not playing better. He trained so hard, but he was putting a lot of pressure on himself. He expected perfection in every game, but was far from it. He hadn't been this uncertain about basketball since the last game of his freshman year. Even though others thought he was playing well, he was becoming more and more depressed.

One evening Mrs. Harding was driving CJ home from a tournament in Ann Arbor and said to him, "You've come such a long way, honey. Why are you putting so much pressure on yourself?"

Raising his voice CJ replied, "Mom, I'm not good enough. I'm not where I need to be. I have high expectations and specific goals and I'm not there yet. Dad was way ahead of me at this point in his career."

Mrs. Harding looked back at her son and said, "Don't be so hard on yourself. Your dad was good, but so are you. It's not fair to compare yourself to him." CJ politely nodded, turned his music on, and slept the rest of the way home dreaming about his future.

Although CJ was upset about his play in the recent AAU tournaments, he was still goal-driven and visualized success on a nightly basis. He continued to work out, transform his body into that of an elite athlete, eat the right foods, and stay away from trouble. He was also proud of the fact that he was becoming a great team player. He was not going to let what happened last season occur ever again.

Not only was CJ focused on ensuring his junior year would be one to remember, he also desperately wanted to become a member of a legacy team. To do so, he kept reading his dad's notebook to see if there was any last minute advice he could receive before his junior year began.

CJ reread the education section and then skipped around from the leadership to the integrity sections and then back to the importance of being a great teammate in life. He was now ready for his final lesson on what it means to be elite. The last "E" stood for **excellence.**

As CJ continued to read, he began to realize the difference between excellence and perfection. His dad wrote, "Excellence is a mindset. It is the idea of being better this year than you were last year, better this month than you were last month, better this week than you were last week, and better today than you were yesterday."

CJ started to realize that excellence was not about perfection but instead a process or a journey of doing your best. He continued to read, "Elite people take great pride in details and let results take care of themselves." While reading through all of the quotes and poems, he felt a renewed energy for his junior season. CJ also took detailed notes and highlighted where his dad quoted Mr. Terry Orlick's seven reminders for excellence, which were:

1. Only Positive Thoughts
2. Only Positive Images
3. Always Lessons
4. Always "I Can"
5. Always Opportunities
6. Always Focused
7. Step by Step

CJ thought back to his AAU games and felt he was putting too much pressure on himself. He didn't feel free to play the way he wanted. He was letting his own high expectations get the better of him. Instead, he decided to quit worrying about results and control what he could control. He would simply do the very best he could. Feeling relieved, he was more motivated now, than ever before.

CJ really enjoyed the section of his dad's notebook that discussed self-talk and the ways in which it leads to excellence. He had no idea how important this was. His dad also had much to write on mental conditioning. He wrote, "People talk to themselves anywhere from 300 to 1,000 words per minute at the subconscious level. Most mediocre people tend to be negative. It is important for military officers to repeat positive affirmations before going into battle. Everything you say should be positive."

His dad also broke down the importance of breathing. "Shallow breathing can lead to a lack of energy and can cause anxiety. Be sure to breathe from your diaphragm before any stressful situation." His dad continued by writing, "Deep breaths and positive thinking can make the difference between living and dying, or winning and losing."

CJ then reflected on his mental game during competition. His body language had improved and he was more confident than ever, but he still had a tendency to be really hard on himself. Before a free throw, he would occasionally breathe really fast and think, "Don't leave it short." According to his dad, everything you say and think should be positive. CJ was amazed how people actually talk to themselves at the subconscious level. He thought about his free throw routine. Although he had made 80 percent of his free throws last season, he knew there was room for improvement. To do so, he committed himself to becoming more positive whenever he practiced his routine.

He continued to read about the path of excellence, and how important it is to not compare oneself to others. CJ thought again that his dad was writing this section just for him. He compared himself to others all of the time. Who had higher grades than him? Who scored more than him? He was even jealous of the bandleader who had more Twitter followers than he did.

However, CJ knew deep down that constantly comparing himself to his dad was the main factor that held him back from reaching his full potential.

No matter how much growth he had shown, in his heart, he still felt that he did not measure up to his dad. How could he? His dad is a legend who left behind an incredible legacy.

CJ had completed his dad's notes, though he chose to reread sections of them every day. He was committed to being an elite person during his junior year and focused on education, leadership, integrity, team, and excellence. CJ still had his note card with the word elite taped to his bedside table. He also created a vision board of his goals and dreams, and he placed them on his mirror which he looked at every day.

The summer was winding down and the AAU season was finally over. After shooting baskets with Tommy, CJ came into the house looking for food. He saw that his mom had a funny look on her face and asked, "Hey, Mom. What's up?"

As Mrs. Harding showed CJ an envelope, she said, "I have an interesting invitation here." She paused and continued, saying, "I held on to this, not knowing what your AAU season would look like or even if you would want to attend. But since you have a few days off, this might work."

"An invitation to what?" CJ questioned with curiosity.

"Well, West Point is having a 25 year anniversary for your dad's basketball team, and we received an invitation. We have not been there in years, and I thought it'd be fun."

CJ looked at her as he grabbed some grapes from the refrigerator and said, "Sure. I'll go. It sounds like a good time."

Mrs. Harding just looked at him with a smile and said, "Great. We leave tomorrow. Your sister has already started packing."

West Point was a little over 12 hours away from Michigan. Mrs. Harding loved their time together. Between her work schedule, CJ's basketball, and Katie's gymnastics, they rarely had time for just the three of them to talk amongst themselves. The car ride would give them an opportunity to just hangout as a family. This was true family bonding. CJ was riding shotgun and staring out of the window, seemingly lost in thought. He eventually asked his mother, "Do you think Coach Taylor will be at the reunion?"

Mrs. Harding replied in a thoughtful manner. "I'm not sure, CJ. He's a very busy man. I do know your daddy's team was one of his favorites. I sure hope he shows up. I just love that man. Your daddy thought the world of him."

CJ could not figure Coach Taylor out. He was sort of an enigma. You could not Google his name without seeing a YouTube clip of him throwing his jacket, screaming at an official, or berating the media for asking a stupid question. Yet his dad, who everyone said was so polite and perfect, seemed to really love him. Even his mom thought he was a great guy.

Coach Taylor retired from coaching with more wins than anyone who had ever coached. He won five NCAA championships and coached the USA basketball team to an Olympic gold medal. He also wrote two very successful books on leadership and was in high demand as a motivational speaker. Since retiring from coaching, he had been working as a color commentator for a popular sports network. CJ hoped to see Coach Taylor again, but was not counting on it.

The Hardings arrived at their hotel which was located just a few miles away from West Point. They had time to shower and freshen up before the dinner and ceremony. CJ could barely remember the last time they were at West Point. As they drove through campus, he stared out of the window at the historic surroundings in amazement. Katie enthusiastically bellowed, "We are finally here!"

West Point was an immaculate place that exuded excellence. As they drove through campus, they passed all the great statues of the famous alumni and legacy leaders. Through his studies and readings, CJ knew many of the important generals from the Civil War, including Grant, Lee, Stonewall Jackson, and Sherman. He also knew the standout generals from the 20th century, such as Pershing, MacArthur, Patton, and Eisenhower. Like his dad, CJ enjoyed reading about what separated the great men from everyone else.

CJ also had time to reflect on what it meant to be elite. He thought of his dad, and how much he loved West Point. CJ also noticed how meticulous the grounds on campus looked. It was a beautiful August day, and even the most casual observer could notice the attention to detail. The cadets were also impossible to ignore. They walked through campus and carried themselves with such confidence and certainty. It was a sight to see.

West Point officers exemplified excellence in everything they did, from the way they walked to the shine in their shoes. As CJ observed the cadets, he remembered his father's notes about the importance of body language and that everything you do sends a message.

They arrived at the banquet hall and were greeted at the door by a few cadets. They checked in, and instantly a few former teammates of CJ's dad recognized Mrs. Harding. CJ had always admired his mom, but this was the first time he realized how beautiful she really was. It was not hard to understand why his dad fell in love with her so many years ago. She was thrilled to see so many old friends, and CJ could not have been happier for her. While his mom was busy catching up, CJ grabbed Katie's hand and started looking for their seat. The surroundings were very impressive. This turned out to be a much bigger celebration than he had anticipated.

The Hardings shared a table with one of his dad's favorite teammates, Mr. Dockish, or Mr. D as he liked to be called. CJ had met Mr. D a few times before, but he was too young to have had a real conversation with him. Mr. D would always send the Hardings a Christmas card and check in with Mrs. Harding occasionally. He was an imposing man with a firm handshake and looked CJ right in the eye as he said hello. He was the CEO of a very large advertising company in Dallas, Texas, and he had a striking balance of confidence and humility. He wore an impeccable suit as well as shoes that shined perfectly.

Mr. D brought his wife and youngest daughter Amanda with him. Amanda was 16 years old and a junior, just like CJ. Mr. D and CJ spent some time together, and CJ told him all about his team back in Michigan and his hopes for a great season. A great conversationalist, Mr. D was quite curious about CJ and his plans for the future. He could not believe how much CJ reminded him of Chad and felt like he was back in time talking to Chad himself.

Remembering his dad's words regarding the importance of curiosity and asking thoughtful questions, CJ showed an interest in Mr. D's advertising company. After Mr. D explained how his company operated, CJ then asked, "What is the most important aspect of advertising?"

Mr. D smiled as he put his hand on CJ's shoulder. He said, "The most important aspect for any product is to build a great brand name. When people think of your product, they should think of excellence."

He then gave CJ advice about creating his own personal brand name. Mr. D continued, "You are the CEO of your own life. As a young basketball recruit, you should be committed to excellence in every assignment in class, every workout or practice you attend, and even with every person you meet. Ask yourself, what is your brand name? What is the Harding brand name? What do you want people to think about when they hear or see the name CJ Harding?"

CJ listened very intently and learned a lot from their short, yet insightful discussion. He wanted to build a positive brand name – a brand name of excellence.

CJ thanked Mr. D for the great advice and asked, "Do you think Coach Taylor is coming?"

"I'm not sure," Mr. D replied. "He's getting up there in age; but from what I hear, he still keeps a demanding schedule." Just when he thought he had heard every story about his dad, Mr. D told him one he had never heard before. He looked CJ in the eye and said, "You know, Coach Taylor and your dad were very close. During our freshman year, your dad received news that his father had a stroke. Your dad wanted to go home immediately to see him but couldn't find a flight home. Coach Taylor personally took the time to drive your dad home."

He continued, "Sadly, your grandfather died before your dad could get home. Coach Taylor stayed with your dad through the funeral and spent time with his entire family. Your grandparents were not well off and did not have health insurance. Coach Taylor paid for all of the medical expenses and funeral arrangements. It was an incredible bonding experience for your dad and Coach. Your dad always said that he'd run through a wall for Coach Taylor."

CJ thought about how difficult that must have been for his father. He also knew that his grandmother passed away just a few months after his grandfather. His dad lost both of his parents in just a few short months.

CJ knew about the tragic deaths of his grandparents from family stories, but he had never heard how Coach Taylor was there for his dad. Mr. D went on to say, "Coach Taylor was also there for your mom after we all heard the news about your dad. At that time, he was the most popular coach in America, and he stopped everything he was doing just to be there for your mom."

As he put his hand on CJ's shoulder, he continued, saying, "Coach Taylor has a pretty tough reputation; but, if you played for him, he would do anything for you. Loyalty was very important to Coach."

The officer overseeing the event asked everyone to take a seat since dinner was about to be served. While the food was being delivered, there was some commotion coming from the back of the room. As CJ turned his head, he could see Coach Taylor walk in. Everyone instantly stood up and applauded as if the President of the United States had entered the room. In person, Coach Taylor appeared older than he did on TV, yet he still had a glow about him. His presence was hard to explain. One could just feel the energy rise when he entered the room. Coach Taylor simply waved his hands in response, telling everyone to take a seat.

As people finished their meals, the players stood up and mingled with each other before the actual ceremony commenced. Coach Taylor came over to the Harding table to say hello. He blushed when Mrs. Harding came over to give him a big hug and kiss. Coach looked at her and said, "You know,

Sydney, Chad was the smartest player I've ever coached, but the smartest thing he ever did, by far, was marry you."

Mrs. Harding just smiled and said, "You always know the right things to say, Coach. I'd like you to say hello to my children. You may remember meeting them a few years back."

"Oh yes. How could I forget?" Coach Taylor replied.

Katie came running over, stuck her hand out, and said, "Hi, Coach. My name is Katie. Nice to see you again."

Coach smiled and said, "Well hello there, young lady. I wish I had your energy!"

CJ stood up, put out his hand, and with great eye contact and a firm handshake said, "Hello, sir. CJ Harding. Very nice to see you again." Coach looked CJ in the eye and shook his hand.

"Well, it's very nice to see you again, young man," Coach Taylor replied. He put his arm around CJ's shoulder and led him a few steps away from the table. They had a great conversation. Coach Taylor told him some stories about his dad and asked him about his team and how he was playing. CJ told

Coach Taylor about the leadership manual and how much he was referenced in his dad's notes.

CJ was honored that Coach Taylor would spend so much time with him, especially since there were so many people crowding around them, waiting to speak to him.

As their conversation ended, CJ smiled as he pulled out his iPhone, and said, "Coach, would you mind if I took a selfie with you?" Coach Taylor looked at him and raised his voice in a humorous way and asked, "Take a what?"

CJ laughed and said, "You know a selfie." CJ turned his iPhone toward Coach and snapped a picture with them both smiling. It did not take CJ much time to tweet out the picture, "At West Point, hanging with a Hall of Famer." There were a lot of retweets from that picture.

After dessert, a few players came up to the microphone and gave speeches. They honored West Point, their teammates, and praised their coach. They also mentioned how they wished that Chad could be here with them. When the players were finished with their remarks, it was time for Coach Taylor to say a few words. He was a really funny speaker and told a few hilarious stories that had the room roaring with laughter.

Coach Taylor concluded by expressing how much he enjoyed this group of young men. He said, "Of all the great teams I went on to coach and all the great talent I was blessed to recruit, my favorite team of all time is right here in this room." The place erupted with applause. He continued, "This was a team that cared about each other, knew their roles, and didn't care who received the credit." He then recalled the last time the team came together, which was about five years after Chad's funeral. Coach started to break up a little, and CJ looked over at his mom. He could see the tears coming down her cheeks.

Coach finished by saying, "The last time we were together, I had the great honor of meeting Chad's young son, CJ. I told him then what a pleasure it was to coach his dad and this team in general. Though we had won a championship, I still didn't know then if our season together was a success. You see, I never know how successful a team truly is until about 20 or so years after the season is over. Until the day I get to meet your spouses, to see the work you do for your communities, and meet your children who you love so much." He looked straight at CJ and continued, "Well, tonight, I'm proud to say that after spending time with all the families this evening, the season we had together was a great success!" The place exploded in applause, and everyone gave Coach Taylor a standing ovation as he left the podium.

The night was a huge success, and Mrs. Harding was very glad her family made the trip. CJ was glad too. He saw up close what excellence looked like. Mr. D, Coach Taylor, and West Point, in general, all represented the best of the best. They all exuded excellence and had great brand names. CJ continued to use his own personal measurement of excellence, being careful not to compare himself to anyone else. On the way home, he visualized what an excellent junior year might look like, the honors classes he would take, the new friends he would like to meet, and, of course, the upcoming basketball season that was only a few months away.

Chapter 8: Thoughts to Ponder

- What is the difference between perfection and excellence?
- What were your impressions of Coach Taylor? What do you think made him a great coach?
- What does it mean to be the CEO of your own life? What does it mean to have a brand name? Could you explain your brand name to someone else?
- Why do you think Coach Taylor said he had to wait 20 years to see if his team was successful or not? Explain.
- Why did Coach Taylor feel Chad's West Point team was successful? What does this tell you about Coach Taylor?

Chapter 9

Beginning to Trust

CJ felt great pride as he began his junior year. There was an indescribable closeness that he felt towards his father that he never felt before. He had heard so many stories about his dad - as a person, an athlete, a soldier, or a friend - yet, after reading his notebook and visiting his West Point teammates, he had even more respect for him. He continued to reread the different sections of the notebook every night. CJ could not get enough.

As the new school year began, CJ immediately met with Coach Dailey. Even though he was disappointed with the way last season ended, he had a lot of respect for his coach. CJ wanted this team to be closer and remembered what his dad had written about winning and losing. "Most battles are won or lost in the trenches. If soldiers want to stay alive or teams want to win, they must establish trust within their unit."

CJ felt they lost too many close games last year, mostly because the team did not trust one another. Although they had a great conversation, CJ was surprised when Coach Dailey admitted he made some mistakes with the team. CJ was 16 years old and had never once heard any of his teachers or coaches admit they had made a mistake before. Coach Dailey's humility and honesty were refreshing. CJ remembered his dad's words concerning mistakes and failures and the importance of learning from them.

His respect for Coach Dailey was enhanced even further. Likewise, Coach Dailey was impressed by how proactive and mature CJ was becoming. Before he met with CJ, Coach Dailey previously had a long talk with his father about the upcoming season. His father gave him great advice about dealing with parents, handling high expectations, and building trust within a team. He also told him how essential open communication with parents and players is and stressed the importance of developing a vision for the program. Coach Dailey was committed to building a winning culture founded on communication and trust.

CJ ended the conversation by asking Coach Dailey if Tommy could be the team manager. He mentioned how Tommy had assisted the guys with their training, and that it would mean a lot to him to have Tommy become an official member of the team during the season. Coach Dailey smiled and promised Tommy an opportunity to become the team manager.

Even though CJ was only a junior, Coach Dailey nominated him captain of the team. He had never seen someone so driven, focused, and unselfish. Coach Dailey, who was always trying to be trendy, tweeted, "just selected CJ Harding to be captain this year. #focused #worker #leader." All CJ's teammates, as well as most of the community, followed Coach Dailey, so his tweet earned a lot of attention.

Prior to the season, Coach Dailey held a meeting for the entire program. Parents and players met in the gymnasium as the coach explained his vision and expectations for the season. He described his mission statement and discussed what it meant to play in the West Rapids Basketball Program.

He started the meeting with a Power Point presentation, displaying the letters AEO, which stood for **Attitude-Excellence-Others**. These were the exact same three words his dad used during his successful coaching career. In fact, he heard these words almost every day growing up. He just never thought about using them to build his program.

Coach Dailey went on to say, "The mission of West Rapids Basketball is **Attitude-Excellence-Others or (A-E-O).** These three letters will be the symbol of who we are and what we do. This is the **West Rapids Way.** We will begin with an **attitude** of gratitude, which is being thankful for our traditions, the people in our lives, and the opportunities we have. A positive attitude can be transforming and motivating. We will have rising tide attitudes that will lift up all people."

He added, "While a positive attitude can be life-changing, a negative attitude can ruin a life, a team, or a program. We will not tolerate or associate with negative attitudes. We will also strive for **excellence** in all that we are and all that we do. Excellence is a product of a purpose-driven life, with a commitment to be our very best. We will set very high goals and strive each day to reach those goals." He continued, "Excellence is an everyday endeavor and will embody everything we do. From the basketball court, to the classroom, as well as in our homes, West Rapids Basketball players will strive for excellence. We will be young men of high competence and high character."

Coach Dailey continued, "West Rapids players will also be young men for **others.** The well-being of other people will be at the core of our mission. We will be great teammates, hard-working students, helpful classmates, and loving brothers and sons. We will celebrate the successes of our teammates and always look for opportunities to help others in need." Coach Dailey then concluded his presentation by outlining guidelines for parental communication, expectations of the players, and providing an optimistic outlook for the upcoming season.

Mrs. Harding and CJ were very pleased with the meeting. On their way home, Mrs. Harding said, "You know CJ, that was some talk. I'm very impressed. I think this is going to be a great season. I like how Coach Dailey talked more about character than he did about basketball. It kind of reminded me of Coach Taylor's speech at West Point – about how there are more important things than winning or losing a basketball game. Your dad would've really liked Coach Dailey."

CJ couldn't have agreed more and replied, "I'm very excited, Mom. We're not going to make the same mistakes we did last year. I'm captain this year and I'm going to make sure everybody feels that they are a part of this team."

Mrs. Harding was very pleased that CJ was so motivated. She also thought how Chad would have really liked Coach Dailey, and how similar they both were. When they arrived home, CJ taped the letters **AEO** on his bedside table, right next to the word **ELITE**.

Chapter 9: Thoughts to Ponder

- What did CJ think was the main reason the Knights did not succeed last season? Do you agree?
- What was the purpose of CJ's conversation with Coach Dailey? Why do you think CJ respected Coach Dailey more after he admitted he made some mistakes in the previous season? Have you ever had a teacher or coach admit they made a mistake? How did you respond?
- Why is trust such an important aspect of any team or relationship?
- Why did Coach Dailey have a meeting with the entire program? How does the meeting show a change in Coach Dailey? What makes you think it was a successful meeting? Which three words does Coach Dailey want his program to embody?
- How are CJ's dad and Coach Dailey similar?

Chapter 10

Your Decisions Define Your Destiny

The preseason open gyms were exciting to watch. There was certainly more team chemistry this year, and the returning players had improved tremendously. Anthony gained 20 pounds and looked much stronger. He also polished his inside post moves. Carl was also better than ever. His dedication to weight training was evident, and his outside shot was much more consistent.

However, CJ received the most attention. The way he moved on the court was almost magical. He had an energy about him that elevated the performances of all of his teammates. Coach Dailey was in disbelief. He told his staff, "You know, when I was younger, my favorite player was Chad Harding. There was something unexplainable about him. He had the *IT* factor. Whatever that means, he had it. He was so graceful, so pure, and so fun to watch." He paused for effect. "You know what boys? I think

CJ is even better than his dad - if only his dad could see CJ play - that would be something."

The much anticipated season started as expected. The Knights rolled past their first two opponents, setting up a big Friday night game against Derby High. Derby would be their first big test. They were tall and athletic and won their first two games by large margins.

Carl and Anthony started the game running the pick and roll to perfection and CJ was his typical reliable self, hitting outside shots and playing great defense. However, people were most impressed with CJ's newfound athletic ability. He now stood a solid 6'5" and had improved his vertical leap to over 30 inches. He was certainly a Division I recruit, as college coaches not only recruited talented players, but looked for intangibles too. He had great grades, a "rising tide" attitude, a great work ethic, and the physical attributes to play at the highest levels. Many coaches thought CJ Harding was just too good to be true.

The Derby game was back and forth with both teams' offenses at their best. CJ put the game out of reach with a barrage of three-pointers and some clutch free throws in the final two minutes. The

Knights passed their first real test and were excited about their future challenges. Coach Dailey had purposely arranged tougher opponents for their non-league schedule this year. He felt that a stronger schedule would help them become battle-tested before the state tournament.

Though the team was red hot as the holiday break began, Coach Dailey gave the boys a few days off. This was a nice time to spend with family and rest up for a rigorous league season.

The holidays turned out to be the best Christmas that CJ could remember, and, as always, he received a lot of nice gifts. Typically, Mrs. Harding would buy presents for herself and Katie, and put CJ's name on it. However, CJ took the initiative to make this Christmas even more special. For the first time, he actually bought gifts for his mother and sister, who spent countless hours supporting him and attending every one of his games. CJ wanted to thank the two of them for all the support they had given him. He handed Katie an envelope, who responded by sarcastically saying, "Oh, CJ, you bought me a card. How sweet!"

"Just open it, funny girl," CJ replied smiling. Katie opened the envelope and could not believe her eyes, two concert tickets to her favorite band! They were coming to Michigan in a few weeks, and CJ was able to secure tickets from a friend at school. She started to scream as she ran hysterically around the room.

Mrs. Harding looked approvingly at him and said, "That was very sweet, CJ."

"I have something for you too," CJ said, as he pulled out a small box from his sweatshirt pocket. He looked her in the eyes and said, "Merry Christmas, Mom. I love you."

His mother opened the box, and, to her surprise found a locket with a picture of Katie, CJ, and her. The picture had been taken on their trip to West Point, but she had forgotten about it. Under the picture was her favorite quote: "Together We Can Do Great Things." She cried and hugged him, saying, "I just love it. It's perfect."

CJ walked away proud that he had transformed himself in many areas. He was not just a leader in the classroom or on the basketball court; he was a leader at home as well. Leadership was truly a choice.

After dinner, CJ received a text from Carl about a party at Stan's house. Stan was home from college, and he was known for always having big parties. His parents had a cottage in the Upper Peninsula and would often leave Stan home alone. Now that Stan was in college, CJ thought that his parties would probably be bigger than ever.

CJ was an outgoing person, but he did not gel with last year's senior class. He was not really looking forward to seeing them again. They just were not the kind of guys he wanted to hang out with.

CJ remembered reading the section on team, that stated, "It is important to surround yourself with great people." His dad also wrote, "You will be the average of the five people you hang around with the most." CJ wanted to hang around smart people who were motivated, goal-oriented, and thought about success. He liked Carl a lot, but he was worried about the other people who would be at the party.

As CJ listened to some of the new music he received for Christmas, he thought about the party. He eventually texted Carl back, writing, "I'm in."

The next morning, with another day off from practice, CJ had time to read more of his dad's journal. He reread some of the sections on decision making. "Decisions will define your destiny," his dad wrote. He also remembered hearing Coach Taylor say that his dad was one of the best decision makers he had ever coached. CJ continued to visualize. He remembered that the brain cannot tell the difference from a real event or an imagined event. Through visualization, he could train his brain to help him make good decisions. He visualized himself at the party. CJ imagined Stan's house with all the people there. He thought, "What would I do if I saw Derek? What would I do if someone asked me to smoke or drink alcohol? How would I respond?" He spent a few minutes thinking about different scenarios. Visualization helped him calm his nerves and made him feel at ease in all situations.

Stan lived a few blocks away from CJ's house. Since it was an unusually warm Michigan winter evening, CJ and Carl decided to walk over to the party. Cars were parked up and down the street, and they could hear the music jamming as they walked to the front door, which was wide open. They walked in, curious about what they would see. The kids in the front room immediately went over to say hello to the two basketball stars. There was a good mix of college freshmen home for the holidays as well as current high school seniors and a few kids in CJ's class. CJ seemed to draw a crowd wherever he went. Even though he wasn't a party guy, people really liked and respected him. They all congratulated the two athletes on a great season so far and wished them well the rest of the way. Eventually, Stan came over and welcomed them.

"Hey guys. I'm glad you're here. I miss the team."

Stan was actually a good guy away from Derek, and CJ liked him. But he felt Stan lacked self-confidence and did not make good decisions.

"Good to see you, Stan," CJ replied.

"We miss your rebounding," Carl added.

Derek walked in from the back room and smiled sarcastically. "Well, look who's here. The dynamic duo!" Knowing how popular CJ was, Derek tried to make amends. "Hey guys. Sorry about all the crap we put you through. It was just our way of making you tougher. It must have worked, considering how well the team is doing."

CJ and Carl politely nodded and said hello. Truth be told, they couldn't stand Derek, but they tolerated him from time to time. Carl walked into the back room where there were more kids his age, and CJ entertained some of the senior girls with some small talk. Stan came up to CJ and said, "Hey, man. How about a beer? You deserve one, considering the great season you're having." Suddenly, everyone looked at CJ. Not everyone was drinking, but they were all interested in what CJ would do.

He did not hesitate. "No thanks, Stan. I appreciate it. I'll stick with water."

"Come on!" Stan insisted. "What can one beer hurt? It'll probably relax you."

CJ replied, "I'm good, Stan. In fact, I cannot stay too long. I just wanted to stop by and say hi and see how you guys were doing." Stan, not wanting to push things, said, "Cool, man. To each his own."

CJ excused himself from the small crowd around him and went into the back room to look for Carl. He wanted to see if Carl was feeling any peer pressure. CJ could not find him but saw a few kids who were drinking and laughing. He asked, "Have you guys seen Carl?"

Two of the kids pointed outside, while the oldest of the three said, "He went outside on the deck with Derek." CJ, knowing something did not seem right, slid the backdoor open and saw Carl and Derek. Derek was rolling a marijuana joint and about to light it. CJ smoothly walked over and grabbed Carl. Derek looked up and said, "Hey, superstar. Why don't you join us?"

"Hey, man. We have to go," CJ said, while looking at Carl and ignoring Derek's plea to smoke.

Carl was very relieved to see CJ and looked at Derek, saying, "Sorry, man, but I guess I gotta go."

Derek said, "Come on, boys. Live a little. It might loosen you up." They both ignored Derek's last remark and walked around the house from the back porch.

As they walked home, there was an awkward silence for a few minutes until CJ finally asked, "What were you thinking, Carl? Not only is that stuff bad for you, but you could've ruined our season. You know how hard we've worked!"

"I'm so sorry. I wasn't even thinking. As soon as he asked me, I knew it was wrong; but for some reason,

I couldn't say no," Carl replied. "Thanks so much for being there for me."

CJ responded, "That's okay, we're teammates. That's what teammates do. Let's just forget about this and go on and win a state championship." They parted ways at the next stop sign and each walked towards their own house. As Carl walked down his street alone, he felt such relief. He could have ruined his whole season with one bad decision. He was so thankful that CJ was there. Carl was so amazed at how cool CJ was in those situations. He handled peer pressure better than anyone Carl had ever met.

Carl was a high character kid who had a great family, but he just did not have the confidence in social situations that CJ had. Like most teenagers, he wanted to fit in. Peer pressure was a constant challenge at West Rapids High. Some kids made bad decisions and influenced others to make the same bad decisions. CJ thought back to the words of his father, "You will be the average of the five closest friends you have."

Carl was a great friend and valued teammate. CJ was proud that he had the confidence to stand up for Carl, when Carl really needed him.

Chapter 10: Thoughts to Ponder

- What was different about CJ this Christmas season? How has he changed?
- Peer pressure is a difficult challenge for many teenagers. Compare and contrast how Carl and CJ handled peer pressure at Stan's house. Why do you think CJ handled it better?
- Think about peer pressure at your school. How is it similar to CJ's situation? How is it different? Do you prepare yourself to make the right decisions?

Chapter 11

An Attitude of Gratitude

Before the New Year began, the team started practicing again in preparation for the remainder of the season. The practices were very intense, although the three day break seemed to give the players some extra life. The league season started on the first Friday after the New Year, and the team could not have been more excited. Coach Dailey treated each contest like it was a championship game. He scouted each team thoroughly, although he was not a big believer in providing too much information to his players about opposing teams. He wanted his team to control what they could control, to play hard and smart, and above all else, to have fun. CJ noticed that Coach Dailey seemed more comfortable this year. He was in his second season, and this year's team was a lot easier to coach. There were no egos, and everyone rooted for one another. CJ could tell his coach was having a lot more fun this year as well, and so was he. The team also benefited from having Tommy in the program as his interest in the team, especially their stats, lifted everyone's spirits.

The basketball season can be very long, and it can be difficult to stay motivated. One day, after a tough practice, Coach Dailey spoke to the team about how important Tommy was to the program. He also mentioned how blessed everyone on the team was. He emphasized that they should be thankful to be part of such a special team and for being able to play such a great game. He ended by saying, "A team that shows gratitude will be a team that stays motivated, and a team that's motivated is a team that's hard to beat. Let's stay grateful and let's stay motivated."

CJ was impressed with Coach Dailey's talk, thinking it was something his dad might have said. He was certainly thankful to have Tommy in the program and to have a mentor like Coach Dailey.

After Coach Dailey's talk, CJ took time to work on his free throw shooting. He was the only one in the gym. As he shot, he visualized being at the free throw line at the end of a game, making the game-winning shot. Soon Coach Dailey's dad walked into the gym and started rebounding for him.

Coach Dailey's dad often came to the games and would occasionally attend practices to talk to the team or just watch them play. He was very proud of his son and wanted to support him any way he could. Coach Dailey and his father always talked about basketball, and they truly enjoyed being around each other. CJ noticed the great father-son relationship they shared, which made CJ miss his own dad even more.

Coach Dailey's dad was a very wise person. Some basketball experts have said that if he had coached at a larger university, he could have been one of the best college coaches of all time. Although he had good teams, they never were really talented enough to win many championships. In fact, he and Coach Taylor's West Point teams used to play each other every year, but that rivalry ended when Coach Taylor moved on to a bigger university.

Coach Dailey's dad and CJ started talking about basketball, life, and, of course, CJ's dad. "You know, CJ, I recruited your dad for two years to come to my school. I thought I had him. I thought a local hero wouldn't pass up an opportunity to play for his hometown college. It was the biggest recruiting loss of my career when your father decided to go to West Point."

He continued, "I remember that phone call like it was yesterday. Your dad called, and like the gentleman he was, thanked me for all the interest I had in him, but said that he had chosen to go to West Point Academy. He wanted to serve his country and be part of something greater than himself. How could I argue? Plus, I knew he was going to play for a great coach in Coach Taylor. I remember a few years ago seeing Coach Taylor at his Hall of Fame induction ceremony. You know what he said to me?" CJ looked with greater interest, shaking his head no. Coach added, "'If Chad Harding had decided to play for you, instead of attending West Point, you'd be the one giving this speech tonight.' Coach Taylor credits your dad, more than anyone else, for helping his career. He always had unbelievable gratitude for what your dad did for him. The great coaches show gratitude. I know my son appreciates all you do for this team, CJ. You're a special young man. Keep leading this team the right way and good things will happen."

CJ appreciated the heart-to-heart talk. It helped him further understand the strong bond that his dad and

Coach Taylor shared. He also appreciated Coach Dailey's dad taking time to speak with him. CJ, who seemed to always be seeking knowledge, asked him what he thought the difference was between the good and the greatest players. The old coach smiled and the two of them walked over to the bleachers to sit down.

"You know, CJ, that's a tough question. My favorite sport growing up wasn't basketball. It was baseball. I grew up in Boston, and I was a huge Red Sox fan. Of course, my favorite player was the great Ted Williams; the last player to hit .400. I would go up to the ball park early before the games would even start just to watch him take batting practice. He had the purest swing in the game."

He continued, "I will never forget that one afternoon. After an hour of batting practice, his grey shirt was drenched with sweat as he walked to the dugout to get ready to play the mighty Yankees. I was about three rows up from the dugout. Being around him was almost magical. All of a sudden a reporter yelled out to him and said, 'Mr. Williams, Mr. Williams, why do you work so hard?' Ted Williams looked over at him with a glare and said, 'Because when I leave this game, I want people to say, there goes the greatest hitter that ever lived.' He then looked over at me, tipped his hat, and went into the dugout. I will always remember that moment as long as I live."

He then added, "Well, I don't know if that answers your question, CJ, but Ted Williams defined greatness for me. CJ, the great ones are willing to pay the price. They're willing to put the time in to be great. Win or lose, they know deep down inside they have earned the right to lose, and they have earned the right to win."

He paused before stating, "Before every one of my games, I would tell my team I want a Ted Williams-like performance. When my teams left the arena, I wanted the fans to say, 'There goes the hardest working team I ever saw.'"

CJ looked at the old coach, while shaking his head in appreciation, and said, "I want to be like that, coach. I want to be like Ted Williams. I want to be the greatest!"

Coach looked at him and said, "That's great, CJ. I've heard about your dad's notebook. You have a plan, and you're following that plan to the letter. It's very important to know what you want in life, CJ." The old coach paused, looked at CJ, and said, "But it's even more important to know why you want to be great."

CJ looked confused. Coach went on to say, "Your father was a great player and, by all means, a man of high character. I was so depressed when he chose to go to West Point. In fact, I questioned whether I should continue coaching. You see, I wanted so badly to coach the best players in the world, and someday coach at a big university and go to the Final Four, and even win a national championship. That was my dream and my dream consumed me. I wanted to be a national champion coach."

"Like Coach Taylor," CJ replied.

"Yes, like Coach Taylor," the old coach acknowledged. "In fact, it was Coach Taylor's first national championship that changed my life."

"How so?" CJ asked curiously.

"Well, the truth was, I was very jealous. I started asking myself, when would my breakthrough in coaching happen? Why did Coach Taylor get all the breaks? I felt I deserved a chance at the big time. It was a real low point for me."

"What got you through it?" CJ asked, not wanting the conversation to end.

"Well, I cannot take all the credit. I had a lot of great mentors that helped me along the way. But the difference maker for me was getting my priorities right. I leaned on my faith and started praying more and asking God for guidance. I stopped being consumed by material things, like a coaching position or a national championship. Don't get me wrong. It's important to have goals and to be driven. In fact, I needed to succeed like I needed to breathe, and that helped me accomplish many goals. But CJ, you have to put first things first."

CJ nodded his head in agreement and said, "Coach, ever since I started reading my dad's binder, all I wanted to be was an elite person. I wanted to be like my dad. I wanted to be someone my mom would be proud of and my sister could look up to. Like you said earlier, I have a game plan, and it's all coming together for me. I'm so close. I can just feel it. But something is missing. I can't describe it. Like there is more to the binder, but my dad did not get around to finishing it. You see, I know WHAT to do, but I don't know the WHY question. That's what I am struggling with the most. Why? Why do you think I found that binder?"

The old coach listened to CJ with great concern. He could tell CJ was a deep thinker and was really searching for some answers. He replied in a thoughtful manner. "You see, CJ, God has a plan for you. And I will not pretend to know His plan, but I can tell you this. It's more important than winning a state championship. Look at me. I lost out on a chance to coach the great Chad Harding, but now my son is at West Rapids High School coaching Chad Harding's son, who has a possibility of being even better than him. Now that's pretty special. Talk about irony, my son is now coaching his son!"

He continued, "CJ, I believe each one of us has our own special destiny. You just have to find out what yours is. And I am pretty confident that His plan for you is more than just playing basketball. Don't get me wrong, basketball is important, but it will be a vehicle to do greater things in life. God had a plan for me, and He has a plan for you too."

CJ was immersed in the conversation. He was so grateful that Coach would take the time to speak to him. Faith was not discussed much at his house. He knew that his dad and mom brought him to church when he was young, yet after his dad died, his family stopped going.

CJ looked at Coach and said, "One thing that my dad wrote in his notebook was that God puts people in your life for a reason. Do you believe that?"

"I do," Coach answered. He then explained, "Some of the people in your life will help you stay on the right path and some will not. Only you can decide what path you want to take."

CJ looked up at Coach and asked, "How do you know you're on the right path? How do you know you're making the right decisions?"`

"Well, you never know for sure, but the best place to start is by asking God. I think of each day like a basketball game. If the game does not start the right way, chances are the game will not end the right way. It's the same way with each day of your life. I make sure the day starts the right way by reading from the Bible or reading spiritual passages."

He added, "I also think of the phrase, I Am Third. This phrase reminds me that God is first, the people in my life are second, and I am third. It also keeps me humble and ready to live according to God's plan each day. Remember CJ, if you start the day the right way, chances are you'll end it the right way too."

CJ really appreciated the talk and thanked Coach for his time. Privately, CJ wanted to be close to God, but he never had this kind of guidance or encouragement before.

CJ later took the time to Google Ted Williams and quickly read about his career. He found it interesting that Williams interrupted his baseball career twice to serve his country during WWII and the Korean War.

Later in the evening while cleaning the kitchen with his mother, CJ had a chance to share the discussion he had with Coach Dailey's father. "You know, Mom, I had an interesting conversation with Coach Dailey's dad after practice today."

"Oh, I really like that man. He's always so kind to Katie and me at the games. He seems like a great guy. He's certainly proud of his son. What'd he have to say?"

"Well, we talked about a few things. He told me about his favorite baseball player and what separates the great players from the good ones. But then the conversation got into faith and God," CJ responded as he looked at his mother.

Mrs. Harding looked up from cleaning the counter and sat down at the kitchen island. She looked at CJ intently and asked, "What did he say, honey?"

"Well, he talked about a higher purpose; that God's plan is bigger than basketball, and I should talk to God more and ask about my purpose in life."

Mrs. Harding listened carefully and was proud that he was sharing his conversation with her. With a very thoughtful tone, she replied, "Well, sweetheart, Mr. Dailey is a very smart man. We, as a family, do need to reconnect with God. Your dad and I prayed a lot together, CJ. We'd thank God all the time for bringing you into our lives."

CJ's mom continued, "But after your father died, I just put a wall around our family, CJ. How could God take such an incredible man like your father from me? From us? I was just so angry, CJ. I shut God out of my life; and I guess, out of your life too. I am so sorry."

CJ listened as his mother became more emotional. She then said, "I do believe that God wanted you to know your father more, and that's why we found that notebook. God is working in your life, CJ. We just need to do a better job of connecting with Him."

CJ went to bed that night thinking about his conversation with Coach Dailey's dad and everything that was said. He felt even closer to his mother and began to understand just how difficult his father's death was for her.

The more he reflected, the more he felt a sense of gratitude for the people in his life. He felt less stressed and knew God was in control. He could only control what he could control and simply do the very best he could. He would leave the rest to God. He also thought again about his dad's words: "God puts people in your life for a reason, and who you become is more important than what you do."

CJ wrote the words **I Am Third** on a note card and put it on his bedside table, right next to the **ELITE** and **AEO** note cards. Before he went to sleep, CJ reflected on all the special people in his life with an attitude of gratitude. He thought of his teammates, Coach Dailey, and of course his father. He was also thankful for his sister, who he appreciated more each day, and his mother, who was the strongest person he knew.

Chapter 11: Thoughts to Ponder

- What was the central message that Coach Dailey gave the team? Why do you think having an "attitude of gratitude" is important? What do you appreciate most in your life?
- According to Coach Dailey's dad, what made Ted Williams so great?
- What is a "Ted Williams-like" performance?
- What does the phrase "I Am Third" mean? What message do you think Coach Dailey's dad was trying to convey to him?
- Why do you think CJ's mom is the strongest person he knows? Do you agree? Explain.

Chapter 12

There is Always One More Thing You Can Do

The Knights continued to dominate games throughout their league season, eventually posting an undefeated regular season record. They were just too good for the area teams to seriously challenge them. Opposing coaches were very complimentary of the Knights, especially on how they executed on the court. Many coaches were amazed by Carl, Anthony, and CJ's individual improvements. CJ had always been a great perimeter player, but this year he was making plays above the rim. One day when he was in the faculty room, Coach Dailey overheard a veteran teacher say, "CJ is a much better athlete than his father ever was. His dad could never dunk and fly through the air like CJ can. The real test now will be to see if the kid can lead his team to a state championship, like his father."

The Knights were practicing very well, and they were excited for a state tournament run. Their loss last year still left a bad taste in their mouths. Coach Dailey also had regrets about last season, but he was mostly disappointed in himself. He felt he let the parents influence his decision-making too much, and he did not do enough to support the younger players on the team. He thought he let the team down. He replayed Derek's father's conversation with him last year and vowed that if anything like that would happen again, he would handle it a lot differently. Team, Team, Team he thought to himself.

The Knights blazed through the districts and weren't truly tested until the Regional Finals. They played a really talented team from the Lansing area. The Knights typically did not face teams that press the entire game, but that night they handled the press fairly well. It helped to have a guard like Carl, who seemed to have eyes in the back of his head. The score was tied with four minutes left when CJ hit a step back three-pointer. On the next possession, he stole the ball and made a transition dunk to help the Knights take a five-point lead, with three minutes left in the game. CJ then hit six straight free throws to close the game out, and the Knights were headed to the quarterfinals. One more win and the team would be off to the Breslin Center and the Final Four.

CJ continued to reread his dad's manual, thinking about the ways in which the word **ELITE** had transformed not only his basketball game, but his entire life. He also spent time reading the Bible and asking God for direction. He thought again about the story of the prince in his dad's notebook. The prince made great decisions because he was destined to be a king. CJ felt he too was destined to do great things. He had a vision, a plan, and the work ethic to get there. Like his dad wrote, "Success is not random."

The quarterfinal game was anticlimactic. CJ started the game like a man on a mission. He hit three three-pointers during the first four minutes and finished the quarter with a tip dunk at the buzzer that brought the fans to their feet. The Knights withstood a late comeback and held on to win. After the game, Tommy told the team that they shot 22 for 24 from the foul line, resulting in a team average of 75 percent for the season. Their hard work during the off-season was definitely paying off. CJ was a 90 percent free throw shooter this season and had made all 25 of his free throws during the state tournament. He was in the zone. Word around the state was spreading about this young man from the western side of Michigan, who had just led his team to the Final Four. The Knights were heading to the Breslin Center.

There was a lot of buzz at school the next day. The semi-final game was scheduled for Friday at 2 p.m., and the superintendent gave the entire district the day off so that everyone could attend. The Knights were slated to play the Monarchs; a team from Saginaw that was led by the legendary Coach Soles. The Monarchs had sent many players to Division I colleges and even had two former players in the NBA. They were loaded with talent and boasted a 25-1 record. Their only loss came in a holiday tournament game against Illinois's number one team.

The night before the big game, as he often did, CJ spent time rereading his dad's notebook. Knowing how talented the Monarchs were, he decided to review the section on excellence and mental conditioning. He read, "Mental is to physical, as four is to one." He then closed his eyes and imagined himself playing in the Breslin Center, leading his team to victory. Visualization was such an important part of CJ's routine.

A huge college basketball fan, he was also aware of all the great players that had played in the famous arena. CJ felt it was an honor to play there, and he was looking forward to the challenge of competing against the well-regarded Monarchs.

The arena was packed with large fan bases from each school. There were also many fans from around the state who were curious to see this young phenom. Some so-called experts thought CJ might be a little overrated. During the regular season, the Knights had not competed against the same caliber of talent as the Monarchs. Also, CJ chose not to play on a high-level AAU team last spring, thus preventing him from being noticed at some of the big tournaments. Coach Dailey often said to the team, "If you are good enough, college coaches will find you. Don't worry about your AAU team, what position you play, or your stats. Control what you can control."

As the team began to warm up, CJ could sense everyone was a little tight. His team did not look good, and everyone was very quiet. He remembered his dad's words on the importance of body language and tone of voice, and recalled one of his favorite quotes, "Fortune favors the bold."

A proactive leader, CJ was not about to wait for a slow start. He knew from experience that he had to do something. He stopped the warm up, motioned to the team to huddle together, and said, "Listen up, men. This is our time. This is our moment. We have trained for this. We don't have to be anyone else but our best selves today. So let's bring our best. From our toes to our shoulders, let's send a message today that nobody trains like us, we are ready, and this is our time!"

CJ had a way of lifting everyone up, mostly because he "walked the talk." Not only was he the best player on the team, he was also a leader with tremendous integrity. When he spoke, his team listened. The team's body language and energy improved for the last eight minutes of the warm up.

The Monarchs were an imposing opponent, with players who were bigger than the Knights at every position. Their best player, senior Damon Jones, was assigned to defend CJ. Damon was a talented athlete who had signed a football scholarship to the University of Alabama. He was an inch taller than CJ and, from the moment the game began, was on him like a glove. CJ did not seem to be bothered by the pressure, but his teammates were having trouble passing the ball to him. The Monarchs jumped out to an early lead and maintained it for most of the first half. Carl was having the game of his life though, helping the Knights lower the Monarchs' lead to six points at the half.

Coach Dailey was calm during halftime and made some adjustments to get CJ the ball. He was playing well defensively and had four assists; yet he was only two for four from the floor. The Monarchs were playing very physical defense, and it appeared that CJ was off his game.

The third quarter began and the Monarchs scored first, stretching their lead. The Knights' fan base was nervous and quiet, while the Monarchs' fans were going crazy. Every time CJ touched the ball, they would scream, "Overrated! Overrated!"

When Coach Dailey called a timeout, he honestly did not have much to say. The Knights simply could not match the Monarchs' speed. CJ, sensing the team needed to hear his voice, said, "We are going to win this game." The team looked at CJ, and he repeated, "We are going to win this game." He then looked at Coach Dailey and asked, "Do you mind if I bring the ball up?" Coach Dailey nodded his head in approval, and the Knights broke the huddle.

Now playing point guard, CJ brought the ball up, dribbled off a high screen from Anthony and drained a three-pointer from way back. The crowd went crazy. What happened next will go down as one of the greatest performances in Michigan basketball state tournament history. CJ scored 20 straight points, including four three-pointers from deep, a couple of jaw-dropping drives to the basket, and six straight free throws. It was an amazing seven minute stretch of basketball. The Monarchs were able to counter CJ's great performance with some incredible plays themselves, tying the score by the end of the third quarter.

The Knights played brilliantly during the fourth quarter. The rest of the team gained confidence from CJ's magical third quarter, and they were matching the Monarchs basket for basket. Anthony made a big put back, while Carl stole the ball and made a layup for a nice conversion, giving the Knights a four-point lead that they never relinquished. The Knights sealed the game with clutch free throws before the final horn blew.

Realizing they had just won, the team jumped up together in jubilation.

CJ was very excited and celebrated with his teammates. He kept repeating, "One more. One more!" He had finished the game with 34 points, 10 assists, and 11 rebounds, recording his first triple-double of the season. Coach Soles, from the Monarchs, said it was the greatest performance he had ever seen in his long career. This was quite a statement coming from a legendary coach, who had coached some great players in his day.

After the game, Coach Dailey sat in awe of CJ's performance. He thought to himself, "How could this kid be so cool under pressure?" He sat next to CJ and put his arm around his shoulder while saying, "Great game, CJ. Great call on bringing the ball up the court. It really made a difference."

The Knights had less than one day to prepare for the state championship game. They were playing the defending state champions, Detroit's mighty Fort Wayne Cavaliers. They were similar in size and speed to the Monarchs, but also had Rod Simpson, who many considered to be the best player in the state. Rod was a 6'10" man-child who had dominated high school basketball the last three years. He was recently voted Mr. Basketball, an award given to the best high school senior in the state.

The teams and their families stayed overnight at a local hotel in East Lansing. CJ was in a room with his mom and sister. After showering and finding something to eat, he went to bed visualizing the state championship game. In the morning, he went downstairs and ate a continental breakfast with the team. This past year, CJ started to become more aware of his eating habits. In his mind, there were two kinds of food: snack food or fuel food. Before big games, CJ made sure he was eating fuel food. He had a banana, eggs, and toast with peanut butter. He wanted his energy to be in full gear for the 1 p.m. game and remembered his dad's words, "Everyone wants to win. Few men prepare to win." When it came to preparation, CJ left no stone unturned.

It was finally game time, and the Breslin Center was rocking. Mrs. Harding and Katie sat in the first row cheering as loud as they could. Before the tip, Mrs. Harding could not help but think how much her late husband would want to be at this game. He would have been so proud of CJ. She knew that Chad's leadership manual had transformed him into not only an elite athlete, but also a great young man destined to do great things in life. Mrs. Harding and Katie were leading the cheers as the game was about to start.

This was a state championship game for the ages. CJ and Rod did not disappoint the sold-out crowd. The game was fast-paced and CJ could not miss. He would make an incredible play on one end, only to be countered by a thunderous dunk by Rod on the other end. Anthony was having trouble matching up with Rod, so the Knights tried to double team him. He was simply too big and strong. The fans were on the edge of their seats the entire game. It seemed whoever had the ball last would win.

The Knights were down two with under a minute to play when Carl and Anthony ran a beautiful pick and roll to tie the game at 67. The Cavs came back down the court and were looking to run a play, but they seemed a little confused. Their point guard nervously dribbled to his right, and not realizing they still had eight seconds left on the clock, took a wild shot from three feet behind the arc. The ball seemed to hang in the air forever, and, as it came down, it hit the backboard and went in. It was unbelievable! The Knights' bench players fell to their knees in disbelief. CJ calmly called a timeout and looked at the clock, noticing there were only six seconds left.

Coach Dailey was prepared for situations like this. He had created a play known as the "Valparaiso," which the team practiced once a week. He was calm in the huddle as he said, "We've run this play countless times. We can do this." Coach Dailey drew the play up on his whiteboard and reviewed everyone's positions.

Carl took the ball out of bounds underneath his own basket. When the referee handed him the ball, he threw a baseball pass to Anthony at half court. Anthony caught it and turned towards the basket. He saw CJ running from his own baseline up the right wing and passed him the ball. CJ caught the ball and shot in one motion. The shot looked perfect and fell right through the net with just over three seconds left to play. The referee on the baseline put both hands in the air, indicating a three-pointer, and, just like that, the score was tied. The crowd erupted in amazement and applause.

Suddenly and seemingly out of nowhere, another referee, who was on the other side of the court, started blowing his whistle and waving his hands. The three referees huddled together and went over to the scorers' table. After much deliberation, the head referee indicated the shot was a two-pointer, claiming CJ's foot was on the three-point line. The Knights' players were devastated, and Coach Dailey was uncharacteristically going crazy.

CJ was stunned. The entire mood of the crowd transformed from hysteria to hopelessness in just a few seconds. CJ looked at the clock and analyzed the situation. They were down one with 3.1 seconds to play, and the Cavaliers now had the ball. He remembered his dad's words: "There is always one more thing you can do in any situation. There is always one more thing." In the Knights' huddle the team was already making excuses and blaming the referees, while CJ was thinking and planning. He was not about to become negative now, especially not during a big moment like this. Coach Dailey told his team, "Switch every pick. We don't have any timeouts left. So when we get the steal, you need to shoot it immediately."

The Knights broke their huddle and everyone took their positions on the court. CJ could sense they were going to either throw it deep or throw it high in the air to Simpson. As he studied the eyes of the in-bounder, CJ remembered his dad writing that elite officers must anticipate and then execute. When the play began, he saw Simpson coming off a screen, believing the inbounder would throw it high to him. CJ broke for the pass. As the ball was in the air, he jumped up for the interception. He came down with the ball and looked to shoot. Suddenly, a Cavalier inadvertently fell right on top of him. A whistle blew as the referee yelled, "Foul on #14." The Cavs still had a one-point lead, but they had just sent CJ Harding to the free throw line with less than two seconds left.

CJ was a little shaken up from the fall. Anthony and Carl picked him up, and he limped to the foul line. Coach Dailey was jumping up and down, calling Carl over to review the situation. He was also waiting to see if the Cavaliers' coach was going to use his last timeout.

Whenever CJ shot free throws, he had an ironclad routine. He began with one deep breath, took three dribbles, added one spin, and said a positive affirmation. He calmly drained the first one – nothing but net. CJ had one of the purest shots anyone had ever seen. The crowd watched the 16-

year-old phenom with amazement. CJ was "in the zone" and ready for his second shot, when the opposing coach called a timeout, trying to freeze the young star. During the Knights' huddle, Coach Dailey - knowing the psychology of his superstar and that no one was more prepared for this moment than CJ - simply said, "Trust your training." The score was now tied. CJ approached the foul line for the game-winning shot. He overheard one of the Cavalier guards yell out, "Don't choke, superstar."

CJ was trained to filter out negative thoughts or words. He remembered his dad's manual and the section on distraction control as he focused on his free throw routine. He wanted to be in this situation. He was prepared for this moment. Above all else, CJ was grateful for the opportunity. He then used the same routine he had repeated thousands of times. He took a deep breath, dribbled three times, spun the ball once, and finished saying a positive affirmation. CJ shot the ball with a perfect follow-through - nothing but net.

The crowd went wild, yet CJ quickly anticipated a long outlet and stole the in-bounder's pass. The game was over and the Knights were state champions. The players were celebrating in hysteria. It was an unbelievable journey for a team whose school had not won a state championship in over 25 years.

After celebrating with Tommy, his teammates, and Coach Dailey, CJ went over and hugged his mother and little sister. The three of them celebrated in euphoria. CJ looked above, acknowledging that this moment also belonged to his father. Speaking loud enough that his mother could hear him, CJ said, "Together we can do great things!"

Chapter 12: Thoughts to Ponder

- CJ used visualization before the semi-final game against the Monarchs. Why do you think visualization is so important?
- During the team warm-ups against the Monarchs, CJ noticed the team was not ready to play and brought the team together for a talk. What is proactive leadership? How did CJ's talk refocus his team?
- During the last seconds of the state championship game, what was CJ's mindset like? How did his mindset help him succeed? What is your mindset during pressure-filled situations?
- How did CJ transform himself from the beginning of the story, to the end? How can you transform yourself to be an ELITE person?

Epilogue

Immediately after the Knights captured the state championship, news spread quickly about the young phenom from western Michigan. A national sports network even included one of CJ's dunks on its highlight reel, and CJ's Twitter followers exploded to over 20,000. As one of the nation's top college basketball recruits, CJ was quickly becoming a celebrity. College coaches from across the country were constantly calling or sending texts to Coach Dailey.

In spite of all the accolades he was receiving, CJ remained remarkably calm throughout the firestorm of press. He often reread his father's words and remained focused on the acronym for **ELITE: education, leadership, integrity, teamwork, and excellence.** He still had his three note cards, with the words **ELITE, AEO,** and **I Am Third** taped to his bedside table. By reading these note cards and other spiritual passages every morning, CJ was able to stay humble and focused, even as the media attention continued to increase.

Although all the attention was extremely flattering, CJ was most excited about a recent opportunity he had received to visit Washington, D.C. As class president, he was selected to travel to the nation's capital for a student leadership seminar, along with two other members of the student council. Remembering his dad's words about seizing the moment and learning from the best, CJ was fired up about the trip and looked forward to attending a roundtable featuring some of our nation's finest leaders. This was something he could not pass up.

He was most intrigued about the opportunity to visit his dad's grave at Arlington Cemetery though. The past two years had been transformational for him, and CJ wanted a chance to be near his dad and thank him for changing his life.

The Washington, D.C. trip was planned for two days, organized particularly around touring the memorials and attending leadership seminars. CJ sat in the front row during all of the seminars and learned a great deal. He met his district's congressman, as well as both of Michigan's senators. CJ greeted them with a firm handshake and a smile. He was surprised to learn they knew all about him and his team's state championship. They all congratulated CJ on a great season and wished him well next year.

Epilogue

CJ asked the congressman and senators questions about leadership. He shared with them his experiences not only in playing basketball, but in student government as well. He told them all about his visit to West Point and about meeting Coach Taylor. They were very impressed with CJ and enjoyed their conversation very much.

CJ loved the energy of the nation's capital and was impressed with how much positive change politicians can make. Though CJ had aspirations to play college basketball and perhaps one day play in the NBA, he went back to the hotel dreaming of working in Washington, D.C. as a senator or maybe even as president. The idea of serving others really resonated with him.

CJ knew he was called to do something greater than basketball. He recalled his dad's words, "Success is not random. You need a game plan." He also remembered Mr. D's advice on constantly building your brand.

Early the next morning CJ and his group traveled to Arlington Cemetery. It was a beautiful spring day, and the walk through Arlington was truly memorable. CJ felt such an overwhelming sense of gratitude for all the American heroes who gave their lives for their country.

Mrs. Springer, the student council representative and chaperone, escorted CJ to his father's gravesite. He was overwhelmed with emotion and fell to his knees, feeling tremendous love and admiration. CJ spoke out loud to his father, thanking him for being the greatest dad a son could ever have. He promised that he would live up to the words in his leadership manual and that he would always put **education** first and be curious about the world around him. He would strive to be a **leader** who brought out the best in others, as well as a young man of **integrity** who lived a life of honor and respect. He would surround himself with successful people and be a great **teammate**, especially to his mother and sister. Finally, he would be committed to **excellence** in all that he did. Before he left, CJ read a prayer from Douglas MacArthur, the great West Point General, which Coach Dailey's father had given to him.

He read:

"Build me a son, O Lord, who will be strong enough to know when he is weak, and brave enough to face himself when he is afraid; one who will be proud and unbending in honest defeat, and humble and gentle in victory.

Build me a son whose wishbone will not be where his backbone should be; a son who will know Thee and that to know himself is the foundation stone of knowledge. Lead him, I pray, not in the path of ease and comfort, but under the stress and spur of difficulties and challenge. Here let him learn to stand up in the storm; here let him learn compassion for those who fail.

Build me a son whose heart will be clean, whose goal will be high; a son who will master himself before he seeks to master other men; one who will learn to laugh, yet never forget how to weep; one who will reach into the future, yet never forget the past.

And after all these things are his, add, I pray, enough of a sense of humor, so that he may always be serious, yet never take himself too seriously. Give him humility, so that he may always remember the simplicity of greatness, the open mind of true wisdom, and the meekness of true strength.

Then, I, his father will dare whisper, 'I have not lived in vain.'"

As CJ walked away, he reflected on the past two years of his life with great pride. He had truly come a long way. Eventually though, his thoughts turned to his future. He could not wait to get back home to his family, his teammates, and, of course, Tommy. He was ready to start training for a magical senior season. With a game plan for success and a deeper faith that he was on the right path, he prepared for his future with unrelenting optimism.

Chad Harding's Notebook:

Being Elite

Notes on Education

- Be curious. The size of your brain can indeed increase.
- Knowledge is power.
- Think big. Have big goals. Write those goals down.
- Don't be afraid to make mistakes. They make you smarter.
- Good things happen to good people who work hard.
- Try big!
- Sit in the front row. Your grades will improve.
- You start life with 100 billion neurons.
- You then create 1.8 million new synapses per second.
- You must practice a new skill within two minutes of learning it, or the newly formed dendrite will shrivel and disappear.
- Your brain is like a big muscle. It gets stronger by working it out.

- A growth mindset believes that one's brains and talents are just the starting point.
- Great leaders have a growth mindset.
- Your dendrites grow from fun and creative experiences.
- Always grow myelin, which develops on the outside of neurons.
- Myelin allows you to become a better athlete, officer, thinker, and leader.
- Grow myelin every day through invigorating experiences.
- Success is not random. Have a plan.
- It's important to set goals.
- Successful people write their goals down.
- Read five books or 1,000 pages each month.

Quotes:

"The best day of your life is the one on which you decide your life is your own. No apologies or excuses, no one to lean on, rely on, or blame. The gift is yours. It is an amazing journey and you alone are responsible for the quality of it. This is the day that your life really begins." - Bob Moawad

"I know fear is an obstacle for some people, but it is an illusion to me. Failure always made me try harder next time. I have never been afraid to fail." - Michael Jordan

"The tragedy in life doesn't lie in not reaching your goal. The tragedy lies in having no goals to reach."- Benjamin Mays

"Genius is initiative on fire." - Holbrook Jackson

Notes on Leadership

- Eye contact is important.
- Seven percent of how we communicate is with words.
- 38 percent of how we communicate is with tone of voice.
- 55 percent of how we communicate is with our body language.
- Leadership is a choice.
- Be a rising tide. Leaders lift everyone.
- Transformational leaders make a difference in the lives of those they lead.
- Transformational leaders make those around them better.
- Leaders never take a day off.
- Leaders have a vision.
- Leaders communicate that vision.
- Leaders are readers.
- Always choose the hard right over the easy wrong.
- "The world is run by confident people." - Coach Raveling

Quotes:

"I am only one, but I am one. I can't do everything, but I can do something. And what I can do, I ought to do. And what I ought to do, but the grace of God, I shall do." - Edward Everett Hale

"Risk more than others think is safe. Care more than others think is wise. Dream more than others think is practical. Expect more than others think is possible." - Cadet Maxim, U.S. Military Academy

"Confidence helps people take control of circumstances rather than be dragged along by them." - Rosabeth Kanter

"People who believe they are likely to win, are also likely to put in the extra effort at difficult moments to ensure victory." - Rosabeth Kanter

Notes on Integrity

- Character is more important than your reputation. Your character is who you are; your reputation is who people think you are.
- Integrity is developed when there is no gap between what you say you are and what you do.
- There comes a time when you have to give up who you are, to become the person you want to be.
- Who you are is more important than what you do.

Optimist Creed: by Christian D. Larson

- You will be so strong that nothing can disturb your peace of mind.
- To look at the sunny side of everything and make your optimism come true.
- To think of only the best.
- To be just as enthusiastic about the success of others as you are about your own.
- To forget the mistakes of the past and press on to the greater achievements of the future.
- To give so much time to the improvement of yourself that you do not have time to criticize others.
- To be too large for worry, too strong for fear, and too happy to permit the presence of trouble.

Quotes:

"It isn't hard to be good from time to time in sports. What's tough is being good every day."
- Willie Mays

"If you heed your fears, you'll die never knowing what a great person you might have been."
- Dr. Robert H. Schuller

"You can't live a perfect day without doing something for someone who will never be able to repay you."
- John Wooden

"Guy in the Glass," Peter Dale Wimbrow Sr.

When you get what you want in your struggle for
self
And the world makes you king for a day
Just go to the mirror and look at yourself
And see what that guy has to say.

For it isn't your father, or mother, or wife
Whose judgment upon you must pass
The fellow whose verdict counts most in your life
Is the one staring back from the glass.

He's the fellow to please – never mind all the rest
For he's with you, clear to the end
And you've passed your most difficult, dangerous
test
If the guy in the glass is your friend.

You may fool the whole world down the pathway of
years
And get pats on the back as you pass
But your final reward will be heartache and tears
If you've cheated the guy in the glass

"If," by Rudyard Kipling

If you can keep your head when all about you
Are losing theirs and blaming it on you,
If you can trust yourself when all men doubt you,
But make allowance for their doubting too;
If you can wait and not be tired by waiting,
Or being lied about, don't deal in lies,
Or being hated, don't give way to hating,
And yet don't look too good, nor talk too wise.

If you can dream - and not make dreams your master,
If you can think - and not make thoughts your aim;
If you can meet with Triumph and Disaster
And treat those two impostors just the same;
If you can bear to hear the truth you've spoken
Twisted by knaves to make a trap for fools,
Or watch the things you gave your life to, broken,
And stoop and build 'em up with worn-out tools.

If you can make one heap of all your winnings
And risk it all on one turn of pitch-and-toss,
And lose, and start again at your beginnings
And never breathe a word about your loss;
If you can force your heart and nerve and sinew
To serve your turn long after they are gone,
And so hold on when there is nothing in you
Except the Will which says to them: "Hold on!"

If you can talk with crowds and keep your virtue,
Or walk with kings - nor lose the common touch,
If neither foes nor loving friends can hurt you,
If all men count with you, but none too much;
If you can fill the unforgiving minute
With sixty seconds' worth of distance run,
Yours is the Earth and everything that's in it,
And - which is more - you'll be a Man, my son!

Notes on Team

- TEAM: Together Everyone Accomplishes More.
- "Selfish people lose." - Urban Meyer
- "It is important to begin using plural pronouns right way. "Our" instead of "my," "we" instead of "I," "us" instead of "me." Remember that leadership on a team is not singular, it is plural." - Coach K
- "Team, Team, Team." - Coach Schembechler.
- Teamwork is all about relationships.
- Together we can do great things.
- No one ever makes it alone.
- God puts people in your life for a reason.

Quotes:

"People want to be on a team. They want to be part of something bigger than themselves. They want to be in a situation where they feel that they are doing something for the greater good."
- Coach K

"An individual has not started living until he can rise above the narrow confines of his individualistic concerns to the broader concerns of all humanity."
- Martin Luther King, Jr.

"Life's most persistent and urgent question is, 'What are you doing for others?'"
- Martin Luther King, Jr.

"You can work miracles by having faith in others. By choosing to think and believe the best about people, you are able to bring out the best in them."
- Bob Moawad

Notes on Excellence

- "Mental is to physical, as 4 is to 1." Bob Knight
- "Excellence is not an act but a habit." Aristotle
- "There isn't a person anywhere that isn't capable of doing more than he thinks he can." Henry Ford
- When you compare, you despair.
- People talk to themselves up to 300-1000 words a minute.
- Positive affirmations are important.
- Shallow breathing can lead to a lack of energy and can cause anxiety. Be sure to breathe from your diaphragm before any stressful situation.
- Deep breaths and positive thinking can make the difference between living and dying, or winning and losing.
- "If you are going to achieve excellence in big things, you develop the habit in little matters. Excellence is not an exception, it is a prevailing attitude." Colin Powell
- "A foundation of excellence lies in self control." H.L Baugher
- "Life is often compared to a marathon, but I think it is more like being a sprinter; long stretches of hard work punctuated by brief moments in which we are given the opportunity to perform at our best." Michael Johnson

REMINDERS FOR EXCELLING: Written by Terry Orlick: *In Pursuit of Excellence*

1. Only Positive Thoughts
2. Only Positive Images
3. Always Lessons
4. Always "I Can"
5. Always Opportunities
6. Always Focused
7. Step by Step

Excellence

Going far beyond the call of duty,
Doing more than others expect,
This is what excellence is all about!
And it comes from striving,
Maintaining the highest standards,
Looking after the smallest detail,
And going the extra mile.
Excellence means doing your very best.
In everything! In every way.
                                        Anonymous

What the Best Do Better than Everyone Else Written by Jon Gordon author of Training Camp
www.TrainingCamp11.com

- The Best know what they really want.
- The Best want it more than others.
- The Best are always striving to get better.
- The Best do ordinary things better than everyone else.
- The Best Focus: master the fundamentals.
- The Best are mentally stronger.
- The Best overcome their fear.
- The Best seize the moment.
- The Best tap into a power greater than themselves.
- The Best leave a legacy.
- The Best make everyone around them better.

An Elite Journey

Build Me a Son
A Prayer by General Douglas MacArthur

"Build me a son, O Lord, who will be strong enough to know when his is weak, and brave enough to face himself when he is afraid; one who will be proud and unbending in honest defeat, and humble and gentle in victory.

Build me a son whose wishbone will not be where his backbone should be; a son who will know Thee and that to know himself is the foundation stone of knowledge. Lead him, I pray, not in the path of ease and comfort, but under the stress and spur of difficulties and challenge. Here let him learn to stand up in the storm; here let him learn compassion for those who fail.

Build me a son whose heart will be clean, whose goal will be high; a son who will master himself before he seeks to master other men; one who will learn to laugh, yet never forget how to weep; one who will reach into the future, yet never forget the past.

And after all these things are his, add, I pray, enough of a sense of humor, so that he may always be serious, yet never take himself too seriously. Give him humility, so that he may always remember the simplicity of greatness, the open mind of true wisdom, the meekness of true strength.

Then, I, his father will dare whisper, 'I have not lived in vain.'"

169

Michigan Elite 25 Core Principles

By Tim McCormick

1. A powerful handshake is a universal sign of confidence and strength.
2. Hold a conversation with adults and ask a follow-up question.
3. Strong communication: You should return phone calls and texts within 24 hours.
4. Courtesy-Hold the door, proper table manners and write thank you notes.
5. Accountability-You are responsible for your success, happiness and failures.
6. Express common courtesy by learning to say thank you, please, and excuse me.
7. Encourage and mentor a teammate or student from a younger grade.
8. Everyone loves a compliment- Make a difference is someone's day.
9. Strengthen your time management with a 3x5 goal setting plan.
10. Improve your grades- Sit in the front row and read 30 minutes a day.
11. CEO Attitude: You are in control of your life, career, and future. Own it!

12. Avoid destructive decisions that relate to drugs, drinking, and violence.
13. Build your brand with positive texts, tweets, and voicemails.
14. Embrace manhood-Girls deserve to be respected.
15. Avoid career killers and peer pressure—Nothing good happens after midnight.
16. Don't believe the hype: You are very good and capable of so much more.
17. Never let anyone outwork you. Focus on fundamentals to achieve excellence.
18. Impactful communication: Smile, eye contact, swagger, and likeability.
19. Lead by example with good decisions, character, and integrity.
20. Your dress code sends a message about your image and reputation.
21. Enthusiasm: Be excited about the possibilities which exist in your life and career.
22. Build a circle of greatness and surround yourself with friends that share your vision and beliefs.
23. Basketball has plenty of runners and jumpers, develop a complete set of fundamental skills.
24. Bounce back ability is a mind-set that you will over-come challenges and obstacles.
25. NBA stands for Never Be Average-Bigger, stronger, and faster every day.

End notes:

Pages 29 and 154-155: Brennan, Jonathan *Choosing A Good Road* @2011 Good Road Publishing

Pages 29-30 and 154-155: Dweck, Carol Mindset: *The New Psychology of Success* Ballatine Books 2008

Page 31: McCormack, Mark, What They Don't Teach You at Harvard, New York Bantam Books, 1989

Pages 41-42: Covey, Sean *The 7 Habits of Highly Effective Teens*, Simon and Schuster 1998

Pages 42-43 and 157: Borg, James Body Language; *7 Easy Lessons to Master the Silent Language*. FT Press, 2010

Pages 80 and 167: Orlick, Terry *Pursuit of Excellence*-www.zoneofexcellence.com

Page 168: Gordon, Jon, Training Camp
www.trainingcamp11.com

About the Author

Michael Massucci has been a teacher and varsity Boys Basketball coach for the past 20 years. He is also an educational and leadership facilitator for Michigan Elite 25, which is reserved for the top basketball players in the state of Michigan. Michael has been trained in the Stephen Covey Leadership Program, completed the Galileo Leadership Academy, and facilitates a Winners' Circle at his school, which hosts successful people from all walks of life. He earned his B.S. in Education from Central Michigan University and holds a Masters Degree from Oakland University in Reading and Language Arts. Michael currently lives in Royal Oak, Michigan with his wife Karen and their three sons AJ, Anthony, and Jake.

Michael Massucci
coachmassucci@gmail.com
michaelmassucci.com

Follow me on Twitter @Coachmassucci

Notes

Notes

Notes